Courtesy: Whaling Museum Society, Inc.

Mark Well The Whale!

THE BEGINNING OF A WHALING VOYAGE
Cold Spring Harbor whaling crews were solicited through shipping agents, recommendations of fellow whalers, newspaper advertisements, and broadsides as above. Good men were always in demand.
(Furnished by Mr. John D. Hewlett, Wilmington, Delaware)

Mark Well The Whale!

LONG ISLAND SHIPS TO DISTANT SEAS

by Frederick P. Schmitt

IRA J. FRIEDMAN DIVISION/KENNIKAT PRESS/PORT WASHINGTON, N.Y.

EMPIRE STATE HISTORICAL PUBLICATIONS SERIES
Number 97

© 1971 by Frederick P. Schmitt
All Rights Reserved

Library of Congress Catalog Card Number: 75-178039
ISBN 0-8046-8097-3

Manufactured in the United States of America

Published by
IRA J. FRIEDMAN DIVISION
KENNIKAT PRESS
Port Washington, N.Y./London

To my wife Marion and my children, whose patience and understanding enabled me to complete this book.

Acknowledgments

This book had its beginning in 1966, late one summer afternoon, when the late Mr. Walter K. Earle, then curator of the Whaling Museum at Cold Spring Harbor, first introduced me to a vast store of unpublished local documents. There were actually three collections, I was to learn, with one, the gift of Miss Elise H. Jones and Mrs. Marguerite H. Jones Knight, forming the major portion of the material. The Jones Collection consists of hundreds of papers, including lists of sails, rigging, gear and supplies to outfit the ships, whalemen's shipping papers, receipts for practically anything, from doctors' bills, rope, harpoons, vegetables and fruit taken at remote ports, to fines paid for the release of drunken crewmen, as well as reports from Cold Spring captains and port and consular certificates from far flung places and manifests for oil and bone sent home during the voyages. There are representative documents—in varying numbers—for each of the nine ships which sailed from Cold Spring Harbor. There is also the small collection formed and donated by Mr. Henry C. Taylor, which includes several papers relating to the organization and early activities of the Cold Spring Whaling Company. This material is unique. Lastly, there are the personal and business letters, bills of sale, contracts, inventories, statements of account and other documents which were loaned by Mr. Dudley W. Stoddard.

The magnitude of the undertaking was staggering and an entire summer and fall were spent at the museum poring over and transcribing most of these papers, some of which were still folded and piled into neat bundles and tied with ribbon and for all appearances had been untouched for a century or more. These collections were the keel, so to speak, of this history.

From this point, my research spread throughout the world. Hundreds of people and institutions responded to my letters and personal visits and in most cases, when able, provided information in one form or another. A few contributed substantially and deserve special recognition and thanks. Mr. Reginald B. Hegarty, who once sailed on a New Bedford whaler, answered numerous queries and searched hundreds of old newspapers for me in his capacity as Curator of the Melville Whaling Room at the New Bedford (Massachusetts) Free Public Library. Mrs. Sylvia Henry, Librarian of the Pennypacker Long Island Collection, East Hampton (New York) Free Library gave generously of her vacation time to have five Cold Spring whaling logs and journals copied.

Mr. Davis Erhardt, Head of the Long Island Division of the Queens Borough Public Library at Jamaica, New York, and his staff assisted greatly in guiding me through their extensive collection of microfilmed Long Island newspapers. Mr. C. Sone of the Hicksville (New York) Public Library processed my seemingly endless inter-library loans with cheerful cooperation and I could not do without his help in this phase. Mr. John D. Hewlett of Wilmington, Delaware, gave me access to his extensive Cold Spring whaling collection. The chapter on Thomas Welcome Roys would not have been as complete without the help, advice and research material provided by Mr. Mitchell R. Sharpe of Marshall Space Flight Center, Huntsville, Alabama, and Mr. Frank H. Winter of the Smithsonian Institution. Lastly, I must thank Mr. Melvin Conant of New York, whose generous encouragement and support was of great assistance in completing this work. Many other individuals and institutions provided material in the research. Unfortunately space forbids thanking each by name, but their efforts are nonetheless appreciated.

Special thanks are due to Mrs. Margaret Smith and Miss Arlene Smith for proofreading the drafts and typing the manuscript in a cheerful and helpful manner. Mr. & Mrs. Andrus Valentine, Mrs. Jane D. deTomasi, Mr. James McCurdy and Mr. Peter Bongo read the manuscript and made a number of valuable suggestions.

I extend my heartfelt appreciation to them all!

F.P.S.

Contents

		Page
	INTRODUCTION	3
I	THE WHALING ERA BEGINS	5
II	GIVE ME A SHIP	13
III	FITTING OUT	23
IV	OFF TO SEA	31
V	"SHE BLO-O-O-WS!"	38
VI	THE WHALER'S LOT	52
VII	TALES OF BRAVERY AND GALLANT RESCUE	68
VIII	SHIP ASHORE!	84
IX	SOME DISTINGUISHED COLD SPRING WHALERS	98
X	MOST DARING WHALEMAN OF THEM ALL	102
XI	THE LONG VOYAGE COMES TO AN END	119
	GLOSSARY	128
	BIBLIOGRAPHY	130
	APPENDICES	138

    I Cold Spring Harbor Whaling Voyages

    II An Act to Incorporate the Cold Spring Whaling Company

    III Crew List for the *Tuscarora*

    IV Outfit of the *Monmouth*, 1851

    V Items sold to Crew, ship *Splendid*

    VI A Typical Whaleship Medicine Chest

	INDEX	145

Illustrations

FRONTISPIECE
A broadside soliciting hands for a whaling voyage

FIRST SECTION
Portrait of Walter Restored Jones
Portrait of John H. Jones
A contract for shipping on a whaler
Painting of Cold Spring Harbor at the beginning of the whaling era
Stock Certificate of the Cold Spring Whaling Company
Portrait of Captain Thomas Welcome Roys
Sketch of Captain Manuel Enos
Painting of the Bark *Alice*

SECOND SECTION
Painting of the *Tuscarora*
Painting of the *Splendid*
Painting of the *Sheffield*
Painting of the *Richmond*
Painting of the *Nathaniel P. Tallmadge*
Painting of the Bark *Monmouth*
Painting of the *Huntsville*
Painting of the *Edgar*

THIRD SECTION
Silver Medal presented to the crew of the *Monmouth*
Examples of local scrimshaw
A toggle iron used in capturing a whale
Four illustrations from woodcuts taken from Peter Dumont's narrative of a voyage in the *Monmouth*
Old salts of Cold Spring Harbor

All illustrations, with no specific credit shown, have been furnished by the Whaling Museum at Cold Spring Harbor, N.Y., to which grateful acknowledgment is given.

Mark Well The Whale!

Introduction

Pity the majestic whale, for ultimately his fate appears doomed. The problem is clearly over-exploitation. Jacques Cousteau, the renowned man of the sea, has said quite succinctly that, "there is more to life than hides, oil, meat, and ivory." Yet, when will mankind learn to control its lust for the cetacean?

Whaling is a brutal trade, and while I do not necessarily condone it, during the nineteenth century—around which the major content of this book is centered—man killed the leviathans to provide illumination and lubrication when there was little suitable substitute. In those freewheeling days he was pitted—more equally than not—against beast. Today, however, we have progressed to an age of harpoon guns, motorized whalecatchers and mother factory ships complete with helicopter scouts and sonar locating techniques borrowed from antisubmarine warfare. What chance has the whale against such predators?

The fact is that today's whalers are so efficient, and the animals are being taken in such great numbers, that some major species, including the mighty blue, the largest mammal on earth, are in imminent danger of extinction. Even the finback, fastest of all of the commercially hunted whales, cannot elude a modern harpooner. Little is being done on a worldwide basis to protect these beautiful creatures. Incredible as it may seem, even the Canadian government had organized, just a few years ago, guided "Whale Hunt Tours," which enabled "sportsmen" to vent their frustrations on the snow white Beluga whales of Hudson Bay.

Despite warnings as early as a decade ago, and efforts of the well-meaning, yet impotent, International Whaling Commission, the wholesale slaughter continues. Meanwhile, the stocks of whales have rapidly depleted to a point now where more whales of some species are being taken than are born each year. In recent years, as the industry became less economical, Great Britain, the Netherlands and finally Norway, which had pioneered modern whaling, have all scrapped their fleets. Only Japan and the Soviet Union continue pelagic operations today, and unless their catches are carefully regulated, several species will, quite unfortunately, go the way of the passenger pigeon.

This, then, is an attempt to recreate the Golden Age of Whaling—not in the light of the great ports of New Bedford, Nantucket or Sag Harbor, but in that of the some sixty-eight secondary ports, ranging from Bucksport, Maine, to Edenton, North Carolina, which had over a thousand ships of their own under sail in the trade. Specifically, this is the story of Cold Spring Harbor, New York, which spawned some forty-four whaling voyages and ranked twenty-fifth among the nineteenth century whaling centers. This was a typical secondary port, with all of the adventure, heroism and tragedy of the thousands of hitherto anonymous whalemen who had earned their places in one of this country's truly formative industries.

F.P.S.
Westbury, Long Island, New York

1

The Whaling Era Begins

To THIS DAY, the small and charming village of Cold Spring Harbor —just 40 miles from New York City—is still reminiscent of the generation during which it flourished as a whaling port. Nestled in one of the many coves along Long Island's rambling North Shore, the countryside is steeped in history. The native Matinecock Indians originally named their village on the west side of the excellent harbor Wauwe-pex. The white settlers called the area Cold Spring, and in 1826 the post office became Cold Spring Harbor to avoid confusion with an upstate village. For many years afterward, however, the village continued to be known as Cold Spring.

During the mid-nineteenth century, Cold Spring was filled with romance. Many well-to-do visitors flocked there each summer to enjoy the stately, dark wooded hills rising from the picturesque, protected harbor. A narrow, winding road led through the village proper, which stood—as now—on the eastern shore of the harbor. The center, at the time the whaling era began, consisted of three stores, a lumber yard and two wharves, which accommodated two schooners and 14 local coasting sloops, as well as other trading vessels calling up and down the eastern seaboard and as far away as the West Indies.

Cold Spring was created a "Port of Delivery" in the Customs Collection District of New York by Act of Congress in 1799. A Surveyor of Customs was appointed and Jacob C. Hewlett held this office for many years. He had the power to enroll and license, enter and clear ships sailing in the coasting trade and the fisheries, including whaling.

By the late 1830s there were some seventy homes scattered over the surrounding countryside, and many of the 500 inhabitants worked in the woolen and flour mills nearby. The largest grist mill, built in 1809, could grind more than a thousand bushels of wheat per week. There were two large woolen mills south of the village. The first was built in 1816 by William M. Hewlett and John H. Jones and the second in 1820 by John and his brothers William H. and Walter R. Jones. These factories were capable of producing 120 pounds of flannel and broadcloth per day. The Jones brothers were proud of their woolens, for they purchased only the finest merino, shorn from sheep raised locally. The wool was usually carded and spun by women in their own homes and only experienced weavers, "men of families preferred," were hired to produce the intricate cloth. But in later years, as foreign competition took its bite, the mills turned from fine fabrics and carpeting to the coarse wool garments the whalers wore. Eventually, by the late 1850s, the mills were to become completely unprofitable.

The Jones brothers dominated the Cold Spring business community during the first half of the nineteenth century. John Jones, who had the greatest influence in the family, was a self-made, scrupulously honest man, who was said to have had a Midas touch. He started his enterprises at age 22, when his father gave him two parcels of land. On the east side of Cold Spring Harbor, John built his first home and a small general store. By 1820, he was operating the two textile mills and in October 1821 wool products from his factories were winning awards in New York City. In 1827, with his brother Walter, John incorporated the Cold Spring Steam Boat Company. They purchased land and built a dock in the outer harbor, so that soon afterward the steamboat *American Eagle* could make her regular runs to New York. In 1836, when the woolen business began to lag, John turned to whaling, which he was to pursue for over a generation.

Walter Restored Jones was more distinguished than his brother John. His curious name, incidentally, was given by custom, to "restore" that of an older brother killed in an accident. Walter began his business training at age eleven, serving as an apprentice in his elder brother William's flour business in New York. He was an ambitious lad who attended school and studied in his spare time. He continued to work with his brother until the firm failed in 1807, when he returned to Cold Spring and the family general store.

Country life apparently did not agree with him, for Walter returned to New York in 1809 and became active in various insurance companies. In 1842 Walter and a Josiah L. Hale reorganized the Atlantic Insurance Company as a mutual company with Walter as president and Hale as vice-president. The new company was an astounding success, rivaling the old Dutch East India Company. Dividends averaged 35 percent from 1844 to 1854 and reached 40 percent three times before 1860, when the firm handled about 50 percent of the marine coverage in New York.

A lifelong bachelor, Walter Jones was accustomed to working long hours. He frequently appeared at the office before 8:30 A.M. and often worked by candlelight until nearly midnight. He was always the gentleman to his customers and friends as well as to his employees. On a sideboard in his office he usually had a big wheel of sharp cheese and plenty of crackers. These were liberally sampled during negotiations, which ended when the applicants rose and brushed a few stray crumbs from their clothing.

In 1854 the company suffered the worst run of losses in its history. This was a disastrous year in which among other vessels, five Atlantic packets, two British steamships and three clippers, including the *San Francisco,* which with cargo was insured for $254,000, were lost. The settlements for the year were $4,500,000 and exceeded premiums by more than $250,000. This terrific strain, it is said, contributed to Walter Jones' fatal stroke on April 7, 1855.

Walter Restored Jones was sorely missed by his fellow New Yorkers. On the day of his death every flag on Wall and South Streets fluttered at half-mast, and on the day of his funeral the streets surrounding Trinity Church, not far from his office, were filled with mourners. Marine historian, Robert G. Albion, acclaimed him as "easily the outstanding figure in New York marine insurance circles in his day."

The three other Jones brothers, William, Joshua and Charles, lived in the shadow of John and Walter. William was interested in the mills, while Joshua helped manage the family general store. Later, Joshua opened a brickyard at Haverstraw, New York, but the venture almost failed and was saved when his brother Charles bought out his interest. Charles, the youngest of the five brothers, owned a brickyard in Cold Spring, and was a gentleman farmer.

By the mid 1830s foreign competition was severely biting into the sales of Jones woolen products. John Jones and a group known as the "Friends of the American System" worked hard to check imports, but their lobbying for protective tariffs failed. Undaunted, Jones decided to put his money into a more speculative venture—whaling—with his interest sparked, no doubt, by first hand reports of the fabulous fortunes which were being made in the whale fishery, some even as close to home as Sag Harbor and Greenport, Long Island.

Actually, whaling was not new to the Jones family, for the trade had dated back to Major Thomas Jones, a former adventurer and privateer, who was granted a license in 1705 "to take drift whales" off the southern shore of Long Island. A further patent was granted to him by Governor Hunter in 1710. It gave him the right to any whale, wreck or fish found between Gravesend Bay, Brooklyn and the western portion of Suffolk County.

In those days, of course, whales were quite common all along the south shore of Long Island. It was the Indians who first hunted the mammals, and they were later instrumental in teaching the trade to the colonists. As early as 1670 it was recorded that, "Upon the south side of Long Island, in the winter, lie store of whales and crampasses, which the inhabitants begin with small boats to make a trade. '. . ."

Whales were so numerous offshore in 1700 that a woman walking the dunes for a few miles from East Hampton to Bridgehampton counted 13 stranded animals and saw countless others spouting nearby. In time, however, these offshore whales were over-exploited and the few remaining were driven from the coast. The whalehunters then decided to take to ships, which ventured further and further into the deep seas in quest for the leviathans.

Cold Spring emerged as a whaling port in 1836, when John H. Jones, reviving the tradition laid down by his great-grandfather Major Thomas Jones, persuaded 33 men and women friends, relatives and neighbors to purchase the three-masted bark *Monmouth* from Boston and outfit her for the whaling trade. Since the owners had no experience in outfitting a whaler, they wisely decided to sail *Monmouth* from Sag Harbor under Captain Richard S. Topping and an experienced crew. After a fortnight of hurried preparations, Captain Topping departed on July 18, 1836, for the South Atlantic whaling grounds and he returned to Cold Spring on April 10, 1837, with a cargo of oil valued at about $20,000. Voyages to the same grounds, during 1837 and 1838, grossed an additional $25,000.

To be sure, these voyages were somewhat marginal, and when *Monmouth* returned to New York from the South Atlantic on May 24, 1839, with a cargo valued at $13,000 a serious problem developed, which was to become the center of a controversy alarming the entire industry. Since 1793, Congress had prescribed that certain customs documents were required to be carried aboard every American whaler,[1] but over the ensuing years the "red tape" of whaling was simplified in practice and certain required papers were dispensed with, apparently outside the original intent of the law.

Now, when *Monmouth* arrived at New York the Customs Collector took issue with her documents and claimed that she was sailing illegally and therefore her cargo was subject to duties the same as foreign goods. He based his actions on a contemporary Rhode Island court case, in which some alleged mutineers were dismissed because their ship had been sailing under incorrectly issued customs documents. There was some heated discussion, so the Collector requested a ruling from Washington. The Treasury Department concurred with him fully, requiring duties on the cargoes of every American whaling vessel which was not properly enrolled and licensed.

Since the customs people had not enforced the law in years, and probably had not done so since it had been enacted, and now would—without the benefit of any notice—there were loud and bitter protests up and down the entire coast. After all, there was a sizeable number of ships still at sea which had been dispatched under the old lax system and virtually all of them would now be subject to duties when they returned to port. Was it fair, they argued, for the government to punish the whalemen for the customs officials' carelessness in issuing the proper documents?

Harry Hunt, the peppery editor of the Sag Harbor *Corrector,* was so incensed that he refered to the situation as a "wreckless piece of insolence." He insisted that the *Monmouth*'s owners "abandon her to the Government, let her masts rot through her bottom, and moor her where she lays, until the day of Judgement—of the United States Court; and if there is a particle of independent honesty left in that court, force the government to disgorge the full amount of damages, created by a gang of *political black-legs.* . . ." For all of the strong rhetoric and protest, the Government prevailed, and the Jones interests reluctantly paid the petty officials a duty of 15 cents per gallon on 25,988 gallons of whale oil and 25 cents per gallon on 2,363 gallons of sperm oil.

---
[1] The law required that an Enrollment, License, General Clearance, Bill of Health, Passport, Sea Letter, Permit to Touch and Trade at any Foreign Port and a certified copy of the Crew List be carried on board every whaler. Customs officials—previous to this time—did not usually issue both a license and enrollment document to a whaling ship.

After initially searching for a ship in Poughkeepsie, New York, and Philadelphia, John and Walter Jones and their associates bought another vessel, the 379 ton full-rigged ship *Tuscarora* from the N. and W. W. Billings whaling interests of New London, Connecticut in August 1837. An old legend to the contrary, *Tuscarora* was a good money-maker for the Billingses for five cruises spanning the years 1832 to 1837. She made her first cruise from Cold Spring in 1837, under Captain William Dennison, returning some twenty months later with 120 barrels of sperm oil and 1,280 of whale oil.

Although these first ventures barely covered purchase and outfitting costs, payments to the captains and crews, they did permit a small return to the investors. But the Joneses quickly reasoned it would be better if they incorporated the venture to obtain financial strength and additional capital. An application to the state legislature to incorporate the Cold Spring Whaling Company was soon drafted by William Jones, John H. Jones, Richard M. Conklin, Abner Chichester, Zophar B. Oakley, Henry Willis, Samuel J. Underhill, Daniel Rogers and Walter R. Jones,[2] who said that they were "desirous of conducting New Whaling & fishing business & the manufacture of oil & candles & or erecting Dock accomodations for the aforesaid business at Cold Spring. . . ." A corporation, they argued, would permit even people of little means to invest in the business and enable them to readily transfer their shares if need be. It would also allow them to gather enough capital—as a group—to invest in more than one ship, thus dispersing the effect of any potential losses.

The New York State Legislature, after haggling over allowing the transfer of existing property to pay for shares in the new company, passed the act of incorporation on March 24, 1838. William Jones, John H. Jones, Richard M. Conklin, John Willis and Samuel Underhill were authorized to sell stock at $50 per share to a total capitalization of $100,000, but for expediency in getting started, the legislature permitted the company to commence business after only $50,000 had been paid in. The charter was to run for 20 years, with the company

---

[2] William, John H. and Walter R. Jones were of the famous Jones brothers family. Richard M. Conklin, a distinguished lawyer and county judge, owned most of the land in Cold Spring Harbor village at one time. Abner Chichester's family owned the Peace and Plenty Inn in West Hills, near Huntington, Long Island; while Zophar B. Oakley was a farmer, politician and one-time postmaster in Huntington. Henry Willis was a member of a long-established family in Cold Spring Harbor. Samuel J. Underhill was a successful farmer, banker, and for many years, Supervisor of the Town of Oyster Bay. Daniel Rogers was a distinguished lawyer in New York City who served as the whaling company's attorney.

THE WHALING ERA BEGINS 11

being managed by a board of directors, which included a president and vice-president.

Curiously, the act of incorporation cautioned that no "foreigner" could be a stockholder or in any way interested in the company, a parochial concept carried over no doubt from earlier days, when Huntington Town[3] passed an ordinance, in 1671, which required in part:

> ... that no foreigner or any person or persons of any other town in this island shall have any liberty to kill whales or any other small fish within the limits of our bounds at the south side of the island, neither shall any inhabitant give leave, directly or indirectly, unto any such foreigner or other town's inhabitants, whereby the companies of whalemen or fishermen may be damnified, except any such foreigner or other town's inhabitant comes into the said company, or any of them, as a half-share man."

Investors bought from one to 65 shares in the new company, which by 1840 still did not have enough capital to commence operations. That year the state legislature passed another act reviving the corporation and reducing the capital stock requirement to $40,000. Then the company was finally able to purchase *Monmouth* from the original individual owners, and in 1841 it bought the *Tuscarora*. The company, it appears, never really earned enough to purchase additional ships, and the other seven ships which sailed from Cold Spring were financed by individuals who owned shares in the vessels.

By 1848, it was evident that the corporate form of management had not been successful, for in April the *Tuscarora* was placed up for sale, with 1,800 barrels, trypots, whaleboats, chronometers and other items from her outfit. Apparently there were no interested buyers, for the ship was subsequently placed on the auction block the following month. There were no bidders, so John H. Jones and his associates decided to rescue *Tuscarora* from the shipbreakers by purchasing her in July, 1848. On December 28, 1850, the company sold its remaining ship, the *Monmouth,* to John Jones' son Townsend for $2,800. In the spring of 1851, with all of its ships gone, the directors filed an application with the Supreme Court of New York requesting permission to dissolve the corporation.

Throughout the period John H. Jones served as managing agent

---

[3] Cold Spring village proper is situated in Huntington Township, while the western portion of the community lies in the Town of Oyster Bay.

for both the Cold Spring Whaling Company and the individual owners of the ships. Walter Restored Jones and Samuel Willets were the owners' agents in New York City. Walter Jones used his wide influence to locate investors and ships for the fleet, while Amos and Samuel Willets, through their ship chandler shop, obtained stores and gear at good prices and sold Cold Spring oil and bone at a commission on the New York market.

The headquarters of the Cold Spring whaling industry was informally located in John Jones' shop at the eastern head of the harbor. For over 20 years, this simple combination general store and post office was the focal point for the enterprise. It was here that the sailors received their outfits after signing on for a two to four year voyage. Every phase of the operations was run from the Jones store, from the initial outfitting of provisions and stores, to the direction during the voyages, to the final disposition of the crews and cargo when the ships returned. The logs and documents, tied with rough cord into neat bundles, were stored in the shop's loft, signalling the end of one voyage and the beginning of another.

2

Give Me A Ship

A YELLOWED newspaper account, dated 1848, boasts that Cold Spring ships sailed "as far on their voyages, as Capt. Cook did, when he circumnavigated the globe." This is fact, for the old logs, now faded and age stained, attest to calls to every continent, save one, and cruises on every ocean of the world in quest for the elusive whale. Several of the ships, including the *Tuscarora* and *Nathaniel P. Tallmadge* actually did sail 'round the world. *Tuscarora* girdled the globe from 1839 to 1841, sailing east to west, by way of the Azores, Tristan da Cunha, the Cape of Good Hope, the Indian Ocean, Australia, New Zealand, Polynesia, Cape Horn and then home. The *Nathaniel P. Tallmadge* made a very similar voyage from 1843 to 1845, except for a four month excursion into the North Pacific.

None of the Cold Spring ships were new, and only the *Nathaniel P. Tallmadge* had actually been built for the whaling trade. The remainder were an assortment of second hand coastwise merchantmen and packets, which included a fast Baltimore China preclipper, a record-breaking New Orleans cotton packet and a famous transatlantic queen. Each of these ships was selected for either one or both of the two essential characteristics: speed and cargo carrying capacity. Retired packet ships made the best whalers, because they were generally fast, flat-bottomed craft. Designed to carry large, heavy cotton bales in the packet trade, they were readily adaptable to the storage of oil casks in whaling. In addition, generally little modification was needed, save for the installation of the tryworks, in which the whale blubber was boiled and rendered, and outfitting with special heavy tackle to handle pieces of whale when "cutting in."

Walter Restored Jones, through his many contacts in the New York maritime industry, assisted in purchasing most of the Cold Spring whalers. These vessels, nine in all, varied in size from the 280 ton *Monmouth* to the *Sheffield,* 579 tons, which was the largest whaler ever to sail out of Long Island and the third largest ship in the industry. Buying and then outfitting a ship for the whaling trade was expensive even for those times. *Splendid,* acquired in 1844, cost $15,000, while *Sheffield,* which was bought the following year for $20,000, cost an additional $20,000 to outfit for her first whaling voyage. By 1848 the ships and outfits represented a total value of $227,000, aggregated 3,272 tons and employed 250 men, representing quite a sizeable investment for a small port.

Monmouth, the first—and smallest—of the ships was built at Charlestown, Massachusetts in 1825 by John M. Robertson. Probably a former coastwise merchantman, she was bought in Boston during July 1836, by John H. Jones and a number of his associates.

Tuscarora was a veteran before coming to Cold Spring. Named for an ancient Indian tribe, she was built late in the spring of 1819 in the Southwark district of Philadelphia by a master carpenter named Robert Burton. Owned by Thomas P. Cope and his brother, Henry, she helped inaugurate their transatlantic packet service from Philadelphia. Sailing under Captain William West, she cleared for her maiden voyage to Liverpool on July 3, 1819, with a cargo of 400 bundles of hoop iron and 20 bundles of sheet iron. Thereafter, *Tuscarora* made some 33 transatlantic round trips under the Cope Line flag, many of them commanded by Captain James Serrill, who first reported aboard in July 1822.

In 1831 Captain Serrill turned command over to Captain J. H. Cheyney, who took the *Tuscarora* out for the last two voyages under the Cope flag. She last entered Philadelphia on April 25, 1832, and was subsequently sold to N. & W. W. Billings of New London, Connecticut, for outfitting as a whaler. She made five voyages from 1832 to 1837 under Captain Franklin F. Smith, a fabulously successful whaling master, who on seven successive voyages managed to stow down 16,154 barrels of whale oil and 1,147 barrels of sperm oil, valued at approximately $650,000. On *Tuscarora*'s return in 1837 the Billingses decided to sell her to the Jones interests, who sailed her from Cold Spring for another six voyages.

* * *

TABLE I
The Cold Spring Whaling Fleet

Name	Rig	Tons	Dimensions (in feet)¹ L	W	D	Approx. Capacity (barrels)	Year Built	Figure-head	Years operating from Cold Spring
Monmouth	Bark	280	100	25	13	2,000	1825	Billet	1836-1862
Tuscarora	Ship	379	102	29	15	3,000	1819	Indian Man	1837-1851
N. P. Tallmadge	Ship	370	108	28	18	3,000	1835-6	Man	1843-1855
Huntsville	Ship	523	131	30	15	4,000	1831	Man	1844-1858
Richmond	Ship	437	118	29	14	3,000	1825	Billet	1843-1849
Splendid	Ship	423	121	29	14	3,200	1832	Woman	1844-1860
Alice	Bark	281	107	24	12	2,500	1830	Billet	1844-1862
Sheffield	Ship	579	133	31	16	3,500	1831	Billet	1845-1859
Edgar	Ship	420	122	28	14	3,500	1844	Billet	1852-1855

Notes: 1. Dimensions rounded to nearest foot.
2. All ships had square sterns, three masts and two decks.
3. A number of authors have stated that *Barclay* (167) sailed on one voyage from Cold Spring in 1839. This has been found to be an error caused by a typesetter in Alexander Starbuck's *History of the American Whale Fishery* (Washington, 1878).

Nathaniel P. Tallmadge was the only Cold Spring whaleship which had been specifically built for the whaling trade. Laid down at Poughkeepsie, New York—some 80 miles up the Hudson River—during 1835 and 1836, she was named for Nathaniel Pendleton Tallmadge, a United States Senator, onetime potential candidate for the Vice-Presidency of the United States, and, in 1833, one of the incorporators of the Dutchess Whaling Company. While it may seem peculiar, Poughkeepsie and the neighboring river towns of Hudson and Newburgh were all thriving nineteenth century whaling ports; the extra hundred miles up-river meaning little timewise when contrasted against a voyage of from two to four years' duration.

The *Nathaniel P. Tallmadge* sailed on two whaling voyages from Poughkeepsie, in 1836 and 1840, before being sold to Cold Spring in 1843. Her first voyage was a smashing success, and steady reports of her proud "takes" appeared regularly in the local newspapers. One, datelined 1838, reported her safe in the Pacific with 1,050 barrels of sperm oil and 350 of whale oil and some whalebone, all valued at $35,000. The 1840 voyage was equally profitable, for when *Nathaniel P. Tallmadge* entered New York on March 22, 1843, she had on board some 2,500 barrels of whale oil, 120 barrels of sperm and 25,000 pounds of bone.

But soon the interest and rejoicing that had marked Poughkeepsie whaling during the prior decade began to wane rapidly. The boastful newspaper commentary appeared no more. The public, it seems, had their fill with whaling, for the panic of 1837 had brought the demise of the rival Poughkeepsie Whaling Company and the industry became a lot more cautious from that time on. Naturally, investors cast a worried look toward the Dutchess Whaling Company; yet despite public apathy, the company continued to prosper.

Dutchess's fortunes were bright and its six ships doing well, when the company declared its second dividend in the fall of 1840. Soon, however, fate turned, beginning with the loss of the *Elbe* off Cook's Straits, New Zealand, in December 1841, which plunged the company into financial difficulties. Then, in a last ditch effort to stave off bankruptcy the company began to sell off assets; land at first, then ships, including the *Nathaniel P. Tallmadge,* which went to Cold Spring in 1843. But even these drastic efforts at raising cash were not enough, for the firm finally went into receivership in 1848. Bankrupt, both financially and spirtually, Nathaniel P. Tallmadge resigned as Senator from New York and accepted the Territorial Governorship of Wisconsin, only to be promptly removed by President Polk. He died an obscure, heartbroken man.

Fortunately the ship bearing Tallmadge's name went on to make four successful—or, as the whalemen liked to say, "greasy"—voyages from Cold Spring from 1843 to 1855. She brought in a total of 8,410 barrels of whale oil, 245 barrels of sperm oil and 53,390 pounds of bone before being sold in December 1855 to Jennison A. Leland and William T. Dugan of New York City, who then operated her as a packet under the Eagle Line flag on the New York-New Orleans run. She is said to have run aground on her first voyage as a packet, but in 1855 the *Nathaniel P. Tallmadge* was rebuilt as a bark and her tonnage increased to 390. Renamed *Norwood* in 1856, she continued with the Eagle Line until sold to foreign interests the following year.

* * *

Richmond was an obscure merchant ship, probably engaged in the coastwise freight trade, which was built in New York City in 1825. She was owned by John T. Farish of New York before being sold to Cold Spring investors for outfitting as a whaler in November 1843. She made only two voyages, one in 1843 and another in 1846, before being wrecked in the Bering Strait in 1849.

* * *

Splendid, the most beautiful ship in the fleet, having been built on Baltimore clipper lines, was a veteran of the China trade. She was built in Baltimore in 1832 and was among the very first of the forerunners of the American clipper ships which gained supremacy of the seas during the latter half of the nineteenth century. It was experience in building *Splendid* and other Baltimore clippers, coupled with the advice and help of the captains who sailed them, which contributed to the development of the great clippers of the fifties. Usually the *Ann McKimm* takes credit as the forerunner of the clippers, but *Splendid* predated *Ann McKimm* by at least a year.

Splendid gained her fame in the China trade sailing under the house flag of N. L. & G. Griswold of New York and in the spring of 1843, with Captain John Land in command, she won her reputation by making the run home from Canton to New York in a very respectable 102 days. But by 1844 *Splendid* and other ships of her mould were being replaced by sleeker, larger vessels. Having served the Griswolds well, she was retired that year and sold to John H. Jones and his associates to be soon outfitted for the North West Coast whale fishery.

* * *

Alice was bought by John H. Jones and associates in September 1844 from Thomas Hale and Joshua Hall of New York and Ebenezer Hale and Andrew W. Mittimore of Newbury, Massachusetts. Undoubtedly the sale was arranged by Walter Restored Jones and his Atlantic Mutual associate Josiah L. Hale. In fact, the Hales continued to own partial interests in *Alice* during most of her career as a whaler. Originally rigged as a brig, then modified to a bark, she was built at Newbury in 1830 and sailed toward the end of that year under Captain Thomas Hale, Jr., with a crew of 12 for the coastwise trade. She continued to ply in subsequent years between New York and Southern ports.

* * *

Huntsville was built in 1831 of live white oak specifically for the New Orleans cotton packet trade by S. & F. Fickett of New York. She was the pride of the firm, which was then one of the major builders of fast coastal packets. Oddly enough, four other ships of the same mould as the *Huntsville,* were being built at unrelated yards at the same time. *Natchez,* built by the rival New York shipbuilders, Webb & Allen, was almost identical to *Huntsville,* but the other three droughers, *Nashville, Louisville* and *Creole,* while basically similar to *Huntsville* and *Natchez,* were slower ships which averaged four days longer per passage.

Huntsville and her sisters were a radical departure from shipbuilding tradition. Most of the coastal packets of the previous decade had single decks and holds which were only 10 feet deep in brigs and schooners and 15 feet in ships, and averaged no more than 300 tons. These older ships had V-shaped bottoms with the keels drawing considerably less water fore than aft. While there was a constant quest for speed on the New Orleans run, and a pressing desire for larger ships, builders were limited by a vessel's ability to cross the shifting bars at the mouth of the Mississippi.

Bucking a centuries-old tradition, the New Orleans packet owners decided in 1831 to develop a better design, since a number of the sharp lined older packets were running aground and having to be towed across the muddy bars. By the end of the 1820s there was a tendency for keels to begin to flatten out, but in *Huntsville* and her sisters the trend was carried to the extreme, so that the hulls were U-rather than V-shaped, providing flat floors and a broad bow and stern, all of which vastly increased storage space for heavy cotton

WALTER RESTORED JONES (1793-1855)
A New York insurance magnate and a leading spirit and backer in the Cold Spring Harbor whaling industry.
(Photograph furnished by the Atlantic Mutual Insurance Company)

JOHN H. JONES (1785-1859)
A leading citizen of Cold Spring Harbor where he maintained the general store and where he was a shareholder and agent for the port's whaling industry for over two decades.

A SHIPPING CONTRACT
Greenhands and seamen, often wharf rats of the worst kind, were sometimes signed on by various New York shipping agents. This contract for three men was for the 1845 voyage of the *Tuscarora* out of Cold Spring Harbor.
(Furnished by Mr. John D. Hewlett, Wilmington, Delaware)

COLD SPRING HARBOR
At the dawn of the whaling era, about 1840. Whaling masters used the steeple of St. John's Church, at the right, to pilot into the outer harbor.
(Photo courtesy of the Heckscher Museum, Huntington, N.Y.)

STOCK CERTIFICATE
Of the Cold Spring Whaling Company. The firm was a failure and many of the voyages were financed through joint partnerships.
(Furnished by the Huntington Historical Society, Huntington, N.Y.)

THOMAS WELCOME ROYS (1816-1877)
Captain of the whaleship *Sheffield* from 1849 to 1854, Roys was one of America's great whalemen. His inventions, experiments and methods were the bridge between the old sail and modern steam whaling techniques.
(Photograph furnished by the Suffolk County Whaling Museum, Sag Harbor, N.Y.)

CAPTAIN MANUEL ENOS
First shipped as a whaler from his native Azores. He later sailed in several ships from Cold Spring Harbor. Enos eventually made captain; sailed out of New Bedford and was lost at sea.

THE BARK *ALICE*
Sailed from Cold Spring Harbor 1844-1862

bales. These hulls were so broad that the ratio of length to beam was 4.4 to 1, giving them lines which were longer and narrower than even the latest Navy frigates.

The new ships readily crossed the Mississippi bar, just as the builders had predicted, but to everyone's astonishment and delight, despite the flat bottoms, they proved, on the average, to be much better sailers than even the most extreme earlier packets. Cotton is a seasonal commodity, so the emphasis in the New Orleans packet trade was quite different from the Liverpool lines, where exact schedules were the rule. On the southern run the accent was on speed, with a fast turnaround, so that the most bales could reach market in season. In off season there were fill-in cargoes and *Huntsville* often carried tobacco, sugar, lead, iron, flour, lard, flaxseed, skins, furs and hides on her manifests.

It was a maritime genius by the name of Edward Knight Collins who carried *Huntsville* to fame. The Louisiana & New York, as it was called at the southern terminus, or New Line, which had been sailing packets regularly from New York to New Orleans since 1823, was acquired by Collins in 1832 and operated under his name. *Huntsville,* which had joined the New Line in 1831, was soon sailing with four other Collins ships on a twice-monthly schedule in season.

As soon as he had gained control of the Louisiana & New York Line, Collins went all out to engage the finest ship masters he could find. Nathaniel Brown Palmer was just one of those great men. Tall, rugged, yet always the gentleman, Nat Palmer, at the tender age of 21, commanding the tiny 47-foot sealing sloop *Hero* out of Stonington, Connecticut, is credited with discovering the mainland of the Antarctic continent in 1821. Soon after he joined the Collins Line, *"Huntsville-Palmer"* became synonymous on the New York and New Orleans waterfronts.

Not long after reporting aboard, Captain Nat realized *Huntsville*'s flat bottom was actually the prime factor which contributed to her speed. He made nine voyages altogether in *Huntsville,* "with a faster average than before or since in the New Orleans service." Northbound, his average was less than 14 days, when most others were taking 18— and in the extreme up to 35 days—to make the same run. While Nat Palmer's name will always be linked with *Huntsville,* Captain John Eldridge, who relieved Palmer, was first to make a record run of 10 days from New Orleans to New York in August 1837. Eldridge, to be sure, was a great captain in his own right, being one of those few

select captains who held command of packets, clippers and steamships.
For her 13 years in the packet service, *Huntsville* ran up an impressive record, averaging 15.1 days on the New Orleans run, with a shortest northbound transit of 10 days and a longest of 28. That record run of 10 days was matched later by 13 ships and was broken by the larger *Silas Holmes* (645 tons) which held the all-time record of nine days. Only one ship, the 664 ton *Sultana,* which entered the service in 1844 and was 27 percent larger than *Huntsville,* beat the northbound average (14.4 days). And not one of the remaining 67 regular New York-New Orleans packets broke these records in the 40 years which comprised the packet era.

With larger, even faster ships—built on the lessons learned from *Huntsville* and her sisters—sliding down the ways, the proud lady of the New Orleans trade was retired and sold on October 15, 1844, to John H. Jones and his associates. She sailed from Cold Spring until October 1858 when she returned to the merchant service. Some 39 years after her launch, *Huntsville* turned up in San Francisco during 1870, still sailing as a tribute to her daring and imaginative builders.

* * *

Sheffield was also constructed from live white oak, with the addition of pitch pine and juniper, in 1831 by the Smith and Dimon shipyard at Corlear's Hook on New York City's East River. At that time Stephen Smith and John Dimon were rapidly acquiring a worldwide reputation for their fine ships. In fact, Smith has been acknowledged as one of the most important of the "second generation" of notable modern New York shipbuilders, and with his partner John Dimon, pioneered in building large ships, combining capacity, seagoing qualities and speed. *Sheffield* was a classic example of their capabilities.

At the zenith of the packet era, four scheduled lines provided weekly service to Liverpool and the competition between them helped vastly to improve transatlantic service. The Black Ball Line from 1824 through 1826 added the large new *Pacific* (587 tons), *Florida* (523 tons), *Manchester* (561 tons), and in 1826 the *Britannia* (630 tons), which was the first packet to exceed 600 tons. The rival Red Star Line was quick to match with *William Byrnes* (518 tons) and *Birmington* (571 tons) which was the line's largest ship until *Sheffield* was added in 1831.

Captain William G. Hackstaff took *Sheffield* out on her maiden voyage and sailed in her until 1834. In the summer of 1836 she was entered in the first great Atlantic packet race by Captain Francis P. Allen, Captain Hackstaff's successor. It was July 8, when the Black Ball Line's *Columbus* (663 tons), Captain Palmer; the *George Washington* (609 tons), Captain Henry Holdridge of the Blue Swallowtail Line; and the *Sheffield* cleared New York harbor with a number of other ships bound in a race for Liverpool, amid high stakes and heavy bets. The three packets remained in company until they reached the banks of Newfoundland, where they were separated and did not meet again until they reached Liverpool. The *George Washington* was first to enter the Mersey on July 25, after a fine run of just 17 days. *Sheffield* cleared only two and a half hours later, but *Columbus* did not arrive until the following morning, because of a slower course taken while searching for more wind.

Then, in the following year *Sheffield* smashed all existing records when she crossed the Atlantic, eastbound, in an amazing 16 days for an average on six consecutive voyages of 17.8 for the 3,332 mile Liverpool run. But her heady success was short-lived, for on a cold November day in 1843, *Sheffield* ended her brilliant career as a packet queen when she was driven ashore in a bitter southeast gale on Romer Shoal off New York. The ship filled quickly and there soon was at least four feet of water in the cabin. Naturally, the passengers were frightened and confused, but Captain Charles W. Popham, half-joking, yet reassuring, calmed them as he carried the ladies—piggyback style—up onto the deck. After 12 nerve-wracking hours in the cold, the 130 passengers and crew were finally rescued by a Staten Island steamboat.

These transatlantic packets were stoutly built, for *Sheffield* was pulled off Romer Shoal, towed into the yards and soon was sailing again in the packet trade. But not for long. Competition on the Liverpool run was keener than ever and the emphasis more than ever before was on speed. *Sheffield* had outlived her contemporaries and was ready to be put up for sale. She was purchased for whaling out of Cold Spring in October 1845 and for 15 years was the largest whaler sailing out of Long Island and the third largest whaler in the country.

* * *

Edgar was the newest ship to sail from Cold Spring, having been built at Brunswick, Maine by Ezekial Thurston in 1844. She was originally owned by Robert and Richard McManus of Brunswick and **Daniel Hood and John B. Brown of Portland, Maine.**

Soon after her launch, *Edgar* entered the New York-New Orleans packet trade, first sailing under the Third Line flag with Robert McManus as master. Then, in 1846, she sailed for the Union Line, Captain Thomas B. Shapter, calling at New Orleans and Natchez. On March 3, 1846, while making the run from New Orleans to New York, she ran aground at Absecon Beach, near Atlantic City, New Jersey, with a cargo of cotton, pork, lard and hams. The crew was saved, but the cargo was a total loss. A few weeks afterward *Edgar,* practically a total wreck, was towed off the beach and into port where she was rebuilt completely.

In October 1846 *Edgar* was again sold, most likely through the help of Walter Jones to his brother Joshua, who promptly sold Walter a half-interest. Another brother, Charles, purchased shares in the vessel in February 1848. The Jones brothers continued to sail *Edgar* as a packet and in 1848 she was operated by the Eagle Line on the New Orleans run under Captain C. R. Smith. She made her last voyages for the Merchants' Line, with Captain George H. Spall commanding, before being converted to a whaler and sailing from Cold Spring in November 1852.

* * *

This tiny fleet of nine seasoned, yet seaworthy ships, subsequently sailed on 44 whaling voyages out of Cold Spring and returned home with over a million dollars worth of whale oil and bone.

3

Fitting Out

WHEN whalers were being fitted out for long and harsh voyages, Cold Spring stirred with activity and excitement. A long, narrow sandspit obstructing the upper harbor necessitated hundreds of casks, barrels, cases and virtually all of the rigging and equipment to be lightered out to the whaleships lying at anchor. At times this inconvenience was avoided completely by outfitting at New York City or on a few occasions at Sag Harbor.

A whaleship was a sizeable investment to risk on cruises to distant whaling grounds and often uncharted waters. A good one cost between $10,000 and $30,000 and the outfits, which included the rigging, sails, equipment and chattels, in addition to supplies for a three or four year voyage, ran at least $10,000 to $20,000 more. At the outset, either the captain or the agent began a list of all the things required for the cruise. There were literally thousands of items to remember, from a ton or two of coal for the galley stove to pats of chewing tobacco for the crew.

Seven hundred individual objects alone were required for the whaling aspect of the voyages, including everything from hundreds of harpoons, spades and lances to trypots, rope and line, heavy blocks and whaleboats filled with gear. Also needed were compasses, charts, coast pilots and the like for navigating, spare parts and hundreds of board feet of lumber for repairing sea damage to ship and boats, as well as enough staple foods to last for several years. As each item was hauled aboard it was checked off in a little notebook and then carefully stowed in its proper place.

When still a young man, John H. Jones made his home over on the west side of Cold Spring Harbor, which at the time was somewhat dilapidated and run down. But Jones worked diligently to improve the place and built more houses, as well as factories, warehouses, and a sail loft and a large cooper shop. Originally, the barrels made there were used to pack and ship flour from the Hewlett-Jones grist mill, but in later years the shop's production was concentrated on the thousands of casks and barrels required for the whaling industry. Because of the barrel manufacture, the area eventually became known as Bungtown, a name which is said to have been first coined during a court case. It appears that a local woman had lodged a complaint of disturbing the peace against a South Seas islander who had just returned from a whaling voyage, and when the judge asked for her place of residence, at first she hesitated nervously, then blurted out "Bungtown," and the name has stuck ever since.

After manufacture each barrel was assembled to check fit, then knocked down and bundled to conserve space aboard ship. Later, on the whale grounds, when the barrels were needed to store the whale oil, the ship's cooper would again set up the shooks, heads and hoops into casks.

Across the harbor the blacksmith busily turned out whalecraft, those implements, such as harpoons and lances, which were peculiar to the whale fishery. The smithy's labor—by today's standards—came very cheap, for in 1844 he charged only 21 cents each for 100 lances and 15 cents each for 216 harpoons. Meanwhile, the village tailor sewed sailors' clothing from the coarse woolen flannel which was woven in John Jones' mills. The several shoemakers fashioned shoes and boots for the whalemen, while local girls were earning pin money making bindings. Even old ladies did their part by knitting the long woolen stockings which kept feet warm in frigid weather.

Feeding 25 to 35 men for months at a time was a major problem. The following list, extracted from a notebook belonging to Captain Henry Edwards, was prepared for the 1854 voyage of the *Nathaniel P. Tallmadge,* and was supposed to provide a basic diet for 30 men for 32 months:

FITTING OUT

90 bbls.	Salt Beef	800 lbs.	Coffee
120 bbls.	Salt Pork	2 boxes	Tea
50 bbls.	Flour	8 bbls.	Vinegar
4,000 lbs.	Pilot Bread	30 bu.	Corn
1,200 lbs.	Medium Bread	2 tierces	Rice
8 hhd.	Molasses	5 bbls.	Dried Corn Meal
7 bbls.	Sugar	1,000 lbs.	Pork
2 bbls.	Salt Mackerel	4 bbls.	Pickles
8 quin.	Salt Cod		

As the provisioning progressed, neat lines of barrelled salt meat began to line the long narrow wharf adjacent to the Jones store. Most of this pork and beef was raised on neighboring farms, while bread and crackers were baked from flour ground in the Cold Spring mill.

It was always difficult to get a good crew, for there was an important distinction in manning a whaleship in comparison to an ordinary merchantman. The whaling trade required, by its very specialized nature, a good percentage of experienced and skilled men to perform labors peculiar only to that industry. Reliable men, who had even cursory whaling experience, were scarce and much in demand. It was especially difficult to lure experienced whalers away from Sag Harbor, New London or other leading ports to berths in old, refitted merchant ships out of such a relatively obscure port as Cold Spring. Most of the crews therefore were recruited directly through broadsides, or newspaper advertisements, through shipping agents, who signed men on and then placed them with shipowners for a fee, and through the Jones brothers themselves, who signed on many men at New York or at the store in Cold Spring. The Jonses personally selected the captains on recommendations and in turn the masters generally picked their own mates and specialists.

The seamen and greenhands who signed on were often a wretched lot in search of either a quick dollar or a bit of adventure. Almost half the crew of the *Monmouth,* sailing in 1851, was illiterate, which was often the rule. Some of the crewmen were juvenile delinquents, drunkards or deranged, while others were wharf rats of the worst variety, recruited by agents in the bars and brothels which lined the New York waterfront. In contrast, however, innocent farm boys—

so young, in fact, that their relatives had to sign for them—often rounded out the complement of greenhands.

Contrary to popular belief, whalemen were not short in height, for the average Cold Spring whaler stood 5 feet 7 inches and even an occasional six footer joined a voyage. He was about 23 years old and the officers were generally young, too, either in their late twenties or early thirties. Generally 17 years was the minimum age for a greenhand, but some lads of 13 or 14 years sailed as cabin boys.

The whale fishery was the first truly integrated American industry. Members of every race—white, black, red and yellow—lived together in harmony more often than not. Most of the sailors were natives of Long Island, including some local Cold Spring boys, but a good many were drawn from upstate New York, New England and the mid-Atlantic states. American Indians, particularly eastern Long Island Shinnecocks, as well as local Negroes made significant contributions to the Cold Spring whaling industry. In addition, a good number of foreign seamen shipped aboard at Cold Spring and overseas ports, and included men from Canada, Nova Scotia, England, Scotland, Wales, Ireland, France, Germany, Portugal, Spain, the Azores, New Zealand and Chile; as well as natives from Hawaii, Tahiti and the Gilbert and other South Pacific islands, all of whom were known collectively as Kanakas. Many of these people could not speak or understand English, which frequently strained the mates' already thin patience to the breaking point.

The number of men recruited, usually 25 to 35, depended on a ship's size and whether she carried three or four whaleboats. By law, every man was required to sign a formal Whalemen's Shipping Paper when he reported to his ship or its agents. This was a contract by which he agreed to perform certain duties in consideration for a lay or share in the results of the voyage. While these whalers generally sailed for a fixed lay for the entire voyage, if a man's work was above average—and he got along well with the captain and mates—he might hope for the remote chance of being promoted to a better share.

The following is a composite of over a dozen Cold Spring crews, categorized by occupation, number of the particular rate who were usually carried on board, respective range of lays commanded and description of their duties:

FITTING OUT

Rate	Number Carried	Lay (range)	Description of Duties
Master or Captain	1	1/14-1/19	Sometimes received other considerations in addition to lay. Responsible for ship and duty to owners to fill her with bone and oil. Served as navigator, disciplinarian, ship's doctor and managed ship's business.
First or Chief Mate	1	1/18-1/26	The captain's right hand. Supervised the sailing and normal operations of the ship. In charge of a whaleboat when in pursuit of a whale, manning the steering oar. Moved forward, switching places with the harpooner, then killed the whale with a lance after he tired. Helped direct the cutting in of the whale when he was taken alongside of the whaleship.
Second or Third Mates	1	1/32-1/60	Generally there was only a second mate, who assisted the first in the operation of the ship underway. Also served as boatheaders, as did the first mate. Responsible for cutting strips from the whale when taken alongside.
Boatsteerers	3, 4	1/40-1/100	Varied according to the number of boats a ship carried. Actually he was the harpooner, and manned the forward oar until the whale was sighted. He then darted the harpoon, changed places with the mate, going aft to man the long steering oar. He was not an officer, but ranked with the other ship's specialists.
Cooper or Ship Keeper	1	1/45-1/120	Also sometimes a monthly salary of say $15. The cooper was a very important and busy man on board ship. He tended and opened the many barrels of supplies and food, utilizing the

Rate	Number Carried	Lay (range)	Description of Duties
			empties and setting up others from the large quantity of shooks or staves, heads and hoops below decks. When the barrels were filled with oil, it was his task to tend them and keep each cask tight. The cooper served as ship keeper, or sailing master, when the boats were down pursuing a whale.
Carpenter	1	1/70-1/180	Another specialist, the carpenter maintained and repaired the ship and her boats.
Cook	1	1/100-1/180	In addition to his lay, he occasionally received a share in the slush, or fat and drippings from the galley. The cook secured the provisions, broke out the food underway and prepared the meals. Helped tend ship when the boats were in the water.
Steward	1	1/90-1/200	Sometimes he shared the slush with the cook. Assisted the cook and served the officers' meals. Some ships carried cabin boys who performed simple chores for the captain and officers.

Note: The following, all considered nonspecialists, assisted in sailing and maintaining the ship; pulled oars in the whaleboats and handled the blubber while the whales were being tried out:

Experienced Seaman	2, 3	1/95-1/200	Generally men who had previously sailed in the merchant service.
Experienced Whalemen	1 or more	1/100-1/180	These men had sailed on at least one whaling voyage.
Greenhands	8 or more	1/118-1/250	Had never been to sea. Got what whalemen called a long lay.

Note: In addition to the above, some ships had Blacksmiths, who maintained the iron work and forged and repaired the whalecraft, and Sailmakers, who made and mended sails and canvas work.

Greenhands had little bargaining power, but experienced men often demanded a good lay and other perquisites before they agreed to sail. Good, qualified officers were in particularly short supply, so they most frequently demanded—and often got—good lays. Captain Jeremiah Mulford, while manning the *Nathaniel P. Tallmadge* in 1845, told John Jones that one prospective mate was only willing to sign for a "27th lay and no less," no doubt because there was ". . . quite a call for Officers at Sag Harbour. . . ."

Sometimes, in addition to his lay, a captain would purchase a share in the ship itself, often paying for it—with interest, of course—out of his lay when the ship returned. Other times he would demand a bonus of perhaps $500 or so if he filled the ship, or ask for $1 per barrel for each cask of more valuable sperm oil that was taken in excess of an agreed minimum. Not so much out of nepotism, but rather trust, some Cold Spring captains induced their brothers, relatives and in-laws to join them. For the ill-fated 1852 voyage of the *Edgar*, Captain Samuel B. Pierson signed on his brothers Theodore as first mate and Elihu as a boatsteerer and his son Charles as a greenhand.

Soon after gold was discovered in California in 1848, many whalemen, who had a basic speculative strain anyway, left the sea and found their way to the booming diggings. After then it became even more difficult—in spite of increasingly better lays—to find experienced whalemen and officers. Sag Harbor was especially hard hit, for it is estimated that no less then 800 of her whalemen left for California during 1849. Captain Freeman H. Smith, writing from that port in August 1849, told of his trouble in trying to locate suitable officers for the *Huntsville*:

> . . . men . . . is very scarce for they are getting up thru Companys for California but there has ben several Portuges to me wanting to Ship but I have Recommended them to go to Cold Spring & Ship. . . .

Most greenhands reported to the Jones store before boarding their respective ships. Here they were given their company outfits, consisting of shoes, shirts, pants, jackets, knives, razors and toilet articles as well as a blanket, cloth, needle and thread, an occasional fishing line and a small ration of tobacco. The outfit would be paid for, with interest, out of the sailor's lay, at the end of the voyage. If a man looked trustworthy he was also given a $5 or $10 cash advance before leaving port. The company outfit was supplemented at sea by the ship's slops chest, or store, where dress and work clothing, foul weather gear, boots and shoes, sewing articles, knives, pipes and tobacco, cloth, shaving articles, cooking utensils and other small items were sold on credit. The slops chest was a lucrative proposition, so the captain would often bargain with the owners for a share or even all of the profits it generated. Captain Edward Halsey netted a handsome $1,232.94 on sales of $2,393.84—practically 100 percent profit —on the 1846-1850 cruise of the *Monmouth*.

From the Jones general store the men made their way to the ships, lugging either a bulky sea bag or heavy chest with them. A few rascals always deserted before the ships had even left home port. When the last few stragglers were rounded up and the deserters replaced, the captain and mates came aboard. Quite often the masters enjoyed the privilege of having their wives and children accompany them for the long and lonely voyages, and some of the wealthier captains, such as Richard P. Smith of the *Sheffield,* even brought along their own paid servants.

Once everything was stowed below and shipshape and the crew was all aboard, the whaler was ready to proceed to sea. Just before sailing time, John H. Jones came aboard and presented the captain with a printed set of standing instructions and an advance of perhaps $250 to cover incidental expenses in the first port of call. The instructions were formal and explicit and were to be followed to the letter. In effect, they officially placed the ship under the captain's command.

The ship was now ready to sail. When the tide was right, she slipped her moorings and hitched a tow behind the steamboat *American Eagle.* Once safely in Long Island Sound, the crew dashed about, totally disorganized, in a confused attempt at working lines and halliards to set the sails and proceed to open sea. For many of these men this was the beginning of a new career in one of the most exciting, yet gruelling and often boring occupations ever devised.

4

Off To Sea

> Almighty God, we pray that thou wilt be with us through our long voyage from our homes and families, and bring us back to them in safety through the goodness of Thy tender mercy.
> Edbert A. Reeve, 3rd Mate, *Sheffield* (1845-1849)

BY NOW the whaleship had cleared home port and was bound on a course for open sea. For at least half of the crew it was the first time they had been out of sight of land. And now those trying days were at hand which would separate the landlubbers from the whalemen. The air was filled with excitement, optimism, apprehension and wonder. "Each of us was fitted out with a complete suit of whaleman's clothes," Peter Dumont, a greenhand in the *Monmouth* wrote, "and felt as though he were already doing desperate battle with some monster of the deep."

"Whaling," Dumont continued, "is about as hazardous and dangerous an occupation as any to which we could have devoted ourselves, but this idea never occurred to our minds, so engrossed were we by reflections on the glories and advantages we hoped to reap ere our return."

By December 1854, *Monmouth* had been to sea only a few days, when Captain Jerimiah Eldredge ordered the seamen to muster on the quarterdeck, where he commenced to lay down the law to them:

> "Now, boys, we're going to look for whales, and I want every one of you to obey your officers in everything you are told to do. If you do so, you'll be treated well; if not, take the consequences on yourself, and don't blame me!"

The whaleships hardly left port when a line of seamen, with faces pale and heads extended, would gather at the bulwarks. Seasickness, oh the blight of the greenhand! One of the *Nathaniel P. Tallmadge*'s crewmen described these poor fellows' feelings exactly:

> Poor boys they are not afraid but wish they were not here . . . but it is no use so cheer up & look forward to the time when your heart may be made glad with the sight of your native land again.

These pathetic 'lubbers, many of whom could do no work, were subjected constantly to taunts and abuse from their more experienced shipmates, who for the most part conveniently forgot those sad days when they were earning their own sea legs. So began the slow and tedious process of molding clumsy landsmen into workable crews. Each had to learn the jargon of the sea, the dozens of lines and the halliards for setting, working and breaking sail, as well as the ship's gruelling routine, consisting of work, watches and work again. Then, each and every seaman would have his turn in the shrouds, clinging, at first petrified, then frightened, at best, to masts and spars wavering wildly some 60 feet above the rolling decks.

Most often the ships sailed for southern waters late in summer or early fall, coincidentally when the western Atlantic is most active, washing the decks for days on end. But the sailors' work continued anyway in salt-soaked clothing and soggy boots and stockings. Each man, while he dared not audibly admit it, longed for a warm, dry spot in which to crawl. Only those who learned quickly enjoyed the privilege of a short, fleeting rest below, while their slower, less fortunate brothers remained on deck, trying to fathom the ropes.

Greenhands generally spent their spare time working; either cleaning ship, breaking out provisions and other stores from the hundreds of barrels and casks which were stowed in the holds, mending sails, or twisting yard after yard of spunyarn, a loosely formed line of unravelled strands of old rope, which was used to tie bundles of whalebone.

By the time that the landsmen had learned the rudiments of seamanship the ship reached calmer and warmer waters. Now it was time to master the trade of the whaleman. The men began to familiarize themselves with whalecraft and the catching gear by watching and helping the boatsteerers fit out the three to five whaleboats. Every item had its place in those narrow, cramped craft. Harpoons and lances found their spot in the bow, oars were placed between the thole pins, and the tubs—filled with thousands of feet of stout, coiled line—and the compass, water keg and a number of other items were secured in the bilge.

Ready for action, the greenhands scrambled into the boats, which were lowered then for the first time. Their first attempts to row in unison might have been laughable save for the epithets and curses hurled on the poor tyros by angry and impatient mates. Sometimes a whale was spotted on the horizon and this provided a bit of realism to the chase, but most often the elusive quarry existed only in the imagination of a tempestuous mate. The practice continued day and night whenever the seas permitted, until each boat crew could satisfy the demanding standards of the officers.

As soon as the wind picked up, the captain would set a course for the whale grounds, the feeding areas where leviathans were likely to be found. The toothed sperm whales were hunted in warm waters, while whalebone, or baleen whales, were caught in warm and cooler climes. Sperm whales have 18 to 30 pairs of teeth in their lower jaws, which they use to seize and devour giant squid in the pelagic deep. The baleen whales feed mostly on small shrimp-like animals called krill, which are strained as the mammal pumps sea water through parallel rows of long, horny whalebone, which line their mouths.

When the Cold Spring whale fishery was in its infancy, *Monmouth* and *Tuscarora* worked the South Atlantic on the Crozet, Falkland, St. Helena, Tristan, False Bank and Western Island grounds. Gradually their horizons expanded and by the late 1830s Cold Spring whalers ventured around into the Indian Ocean and the Pacific in the vicinity of Australia and New Zealand. By 1843 they were working in the North Pacific during the short summer season, cruising the so-called North West Coast or Alaskan grounds, and in off-season sailed on the Australia, New Zealand and Japan grounds. While California was booming with the gold rush several Cold Spring whalers put into San Francisco, and then sailed on south in pursuit of the gray whale which was numerous then in the bays and inlets of Baja California.

Soon, whaling began to center in the North Pacific. Initially, Cold Spring ships concentrated on the Japan Sea, Okhotsk Sea and Kodiak Island grounds, as well as the waters in the vicinity of the Bering Strait, but the whole industry pattern was altered drastically after 1848. Before that time, whaling had begun to decline, and a shortage of labor was developing as significant numbers of experienced men were heading for the lucrative gold fields. But then—almost by Providence—the fishery was saved, so to speak, for a few more decades.

In the summer of 1848, Captain Thomas Welcome Roys, commanding the Sag Harbor whaler *Superior,* over vehement objections from his crew, passed through the Bering Strait into the mysterious Arctic Ocean. There he took 1,800 barrels of oil in less than a month and a half, mostly from the comparatively sluggish right whales, called bowheads, which were abundant there. Although he always received the credit for discovering these whales, Roys maintained until his death that they were first taken by Captain Freeman H. Smith of the Cold Spring whaler *Huntsville* early in 1848 in the Sea of Okhotsk.

Ships bound for the South Atlantic or Indian Ocean usually made their first port call at Fayal in the Azores. After three or four weeks at sea the thoroughly seasick greenhands welcomed a short respite on terra firma while the ship took on recruits: fresh fruit, vegetables and meat, along with other provisions and stores which would be needed on the long voyages ahead. For the time being the men enjoyed a few fleeting hours of liberty, in which they wound their way through the narrow streets of Fayal in search of amusement.

Whalers heading for the Arctic faced the treacherous passage around Cape Horn. Once safely into the Pacific, the ships would call at either Talcahuano or Valparaiso, Chile, and then work on the Chilean grounds, or sail directly to the Hawaiian Islands to recruit for the Arctic season. Several of the Cold Spring ships put into the mysterious Galapagos Islands, made famous by Charles Darwin, for firewood, water and fresh meat.

Hawaii . . . what a glorious sight for a restless and weary crew which had spent so many weeks at sea! Honolulu was generally the preferred port of call before heading for the Northern grounds, and its beautiful harbor was literally a forest of masts in those prosperous days. As soon as the ships came to anchor, the arduous task began of loading fresh stores, repairing damage sustained at sea and outfitting for the season ahead.

By the time a ship put into the first port, the captain usually had made a good evaluation of his crew (and vice versa). The quality of a crew ranged, in the words of the masters themselves, from "cheerful and smart" to "middling" to "children" or worse. After the ship's refit was completed, the crew was placed on port and starboard watches, with half of the men being permitted to go ashore on liberty. They must have been a curious looking lot as they dashed ashore in their best striped shirts, white duck trousers and black leather boots!

At this point the undesirables were dismissed, or deserted while on liberty. Ashore, whalemen were arrested for practically every offense imaginable, but the most common, of course, was drunkenness. If the crime was not serious, the captain would pay the man's fine, which was then deducted from his lay. Many a Cold Spring sailor spent a night or three in the "Fort" at Honolulu, or some other lockup, before his irritated captain happened along to bail him out.

When Captain Hiram Ormesby brought the *Monmouth* into the Azores in September 1857 he reported his crew "all well and hearty and are very good men . . ." that is, except for the cook, whom he was discharging. "I do not think he would be of any use whatever. He can't cook nor do nothing else. . . . I think it will be cheaper to send him home, then it would to keep him the voyage to feed and clothe." Sometimes the captain tacitly encouraged desertion, mainly because an unwanted crewman who ran away, by law, forfeited any money due to him. Captain Hedges of the *Monmouth,* writing to John H. Jones from Talcahuano in March 1844, expressed these feelings: ". . . William Williams I expect will run away shortly or has but will not be missed as he is the only poor man I have got. . . ." During the 1844-1848 voyage of the *Splendid,* 15 men out of the original crew of 31 who had sailed from Cold Spring deserted. It was not at all unusual, for any of the ships, if five or six men ran away in a port.

Empty billets were filled either with experienced whalemen, or with native "Portugees" in the Azores, or "Kanakas" in Hawaii and the South Pacific Islands. The Portugees and Kanakas could be shipped on long lays, because, of course, there was a language barrier, but experienced American whalemen, who had either been discharged or deserted from other ships, would usually demand and get a better lay than they probably would have received if they had signed on back home.

Probably one of the most pleasant aspects of the first port of call, from everyone's viewpoint, was the first taste of fresh food in many weeks. After the initial supplies of fresh provisions ran out, a fortnight or so after leaving Cold Spring, the crew was subjected to probably some of the worst meals ever prepared, consisting generally of corn meal and molasses for breakfast, boiled salt cod, mackerel, salt beef or pork and potatoes for dinner and a poor-tasting thick soup, called lobscouse, for supper. Pepper sauce, purchased from the ship's slops store, disguised the taste. Occasionally, this meager diet was supplemented with ham, dried beans, pilot crackers, cheese, pickles, marinated onions and cabbage and dried apples, which provided some variety. Virtually everything was stored in barrels, which were broken out as required. Potatoes were kept in bins or nets under the boats on deck, and lasted for some time, provided they did not freeze or rot. Many a disgusted crew spent hours sorting putrid spuds from those which were still edible.

The whalemen's favorite beverages, aside from hard liquor, were coffee and chocolate, and an occasional bottle of sarsaparilla. Despite the warnings in the owners' printed instructions against the use of spirits, the captains often had wine and liquor on board. For example, while refitting at Pernambuco, Brazil, in 1851, *Huntsville* took aboard two dozen bottles of porter, several barrels of gin and six barrels of port wine. Alcohol was evident in most of the other Cold Spring ships, and one of them was wrecked while the captain and mates allegedly were drunk.

In foreign ports all sorts of exotic fresh fruit and vegetables were loaded on board, including pumpkins, oranges, coconuts, bananas, pineapples, watermelons, strawberries, sweet potatoes and breadfruit. Lime juice helped prevent scurvy. In the large towns, such as Fayal and Honolulu, provisions were purchased outright, while in the smaller islands, especially in the South Pacific, trade goods, trinkets and cloth were bartered with the natives, who paddled out in canoes laden with fresh provisions.

A number of live animals were carried on deck, and these provided more substantial meat meals on Sundays and holidays. Fowl, pigs and goats were killed and butchered as required. Needless to say, the crew was very disappointed when a hapless pig or rooster was washed overboard, but likewise they were pleased when a hog or goat surprised them with a litter.

Most crews had scant affection for the cook. Quite often he had little or no culinary skill, having just shipped on to fill a billet. After all, he would enjoy a lay comparable with an experienced whaleman, yet would not have to suffer the danger and discomforts associated with actually catching and processing the whales. One sailor in the *Tuscarora,* on the 1839-1841 voyage complained bitterly of the food. This remark, from his personal journal, is typical: ". . . this Day is the first time that we hav had the meat lunch and i hope that it will bee the last for i am sure we hav got enuf. . . ." Certainly, the cook and the steward took the best for themselves. "Sunday . . . fresh hog for dinner and supper but the sturd has told the Chief Mate that sum-body has stolen some of it. . . ." And for Christmas ". . . we have had a very good dinner considering the ingredens and there was Yams and flour and fresh hog. . . ."

Between visits to inhabited places, wild bird eggs, geese, penguins, rabbits, goats, turtles, rock lobsters, crabs, mussels and clams were hunted in the secluded islands of the Falklands, Galapagos and Aleutians. At sea, the officers and crew fished. Some fish were eaten fresh while others were salted and packed in barrels. If they were lucky the sailors might harpoon or hook a porpoise. Though somewhat oily this meat was infinitely superior to the usual fare of salt meat or fish. Isaac Jessup, a harpooner in the *Sheffield,* wrote that ". . . all hands have the pleasure of feasting on Porpoise which eats very well indeed. . . ." The following day, however, they had fresh pork, and Jessup was the first to admit that it tasted better.

By the time the fresh food ran out the ships had reached the grounds and were searching for whales. This period was a time of both apprehension and optimisim for the entire crew. Each man, whether he would admit it or not, was fearful for his own safety, yet at the same time he was contemplating how he would spend his share of the profits from a full ship. A few months on the grounds would tell the tale.

5

"*She Blo-o-o-ws!*"

THE WHALE GROUNDS, neither exciting nor romantic in themselves —these dismal, desolate expanses of sea—were characterized by heavy blankets of fog, chilling cold and biting wind, mixed with rain or snow, for weeks on end. The South Atlantic, North Pacific and Arctic grounds had earned an especially poor reputation for rough weather because continual storms tore at and buffeted the small, leaky ships; flooding cabins, ripping down sails, rigging, spars and masts; with foamy seas all the while sweeping the decks, taking everything in their wake, from whaleboats and deck gear to rails and bulwarks.

Throughout these trying times, frightened men inched along the slippery decks in tarpaulin coats, sou'westers and thick stockings and boots. Tending sails was the most difficult task in a storm, and it was extremely dangerous to bend on a new sail to replace canvas which had been torn or carried away. After several of these beatings by the elements the sails began to look like a patchwork, or worse, and as one Cold Spring captain said, they looked ". . . on the yards like some fast growing Boys trowsers . . . with his legs something like a foot through them. . . ."

One of the *Tuscarora*'s sailors, writing of a particularly fierce storm in March 1840, wished he was home, because ". . . it is rugged and the Ship rowls so that She rowls iron hoops in my bunk. . . . it is the worst gale that we have had on this Voige and i hope that we Shant hav any more like it. . . ." Actually, he had a trifling problem, for it was not uncommon for someone on deck to be injured, or even killed, during an especially treacherous tempest.

At one time or another most of the Cold Spring ships suffered damage or near-destruction. *Tuscorora* was partially wrecked, losing not only several men, but the mainmast (which was shorn off close to the deck), the rigging, boats and bulwarks, in a savage storm some 1,800 miles southeast of the Cape of Good Hope during December 1841. The insurance settlement was over $5,700. In 1849 a gale cracked the knees of the *Nathaniel P. Tallmadge,* and, during a heavy blow in the North Pacific, Captain Thomas W. Roys of the *Sheffield* lost an entire suit of sails plus three of the boats with all of the gear and davits. Then, in 1856, in the Kamchatka Sea, the *Alice* was battered by a fierce squall. Captain George Penney estimated that the damages would run between $3,000 and $4,000 when he reached Honolulu.

In their reports back home the captains continually complained about leaky hulls. Captain Edward Halsey, writing from St. Helena on July 27, 1846, said that the *Monmouth* would have been first rate ". . . if she was tite. She commenced leaking first out. We pump once a day from 600 to 1200 strokes . . . ruff weather she leaks the most. It was something I did not expect. I hope it will be no worse. . . ." But it was a lot worse on the *Tuscarora,* which at times leaked as much as 300 to 400 pump strokes per hour.

When the ships were not being pounded by storms, they were threatened by polar ice, whether in the form of small growlers, bergs or pack ice stretching to the horizon. Encounters by small wooden ships with vast fields of ice were extremely dangerous, and there are numerous instances of individual whaleships, and even an entire fleet, being trapped and subsequently crushed in pack ice. When the *Alice* passed through the Kuril Islands group, off the eastern Russian coast, during the spring of 1860, she encountered strip ice, then, driving north, worked a passage as best she could, taking some rough grinding from the ice. When she returned to Honolulu that fall, her badly strained hull required repairs and new fittings costing about $3,000.

The farther the whalemen drove north in the Pacific, the more they feared destruction from ice and, somewhat exaggerated, at the hands of the native Siberians and Alaskan coastal Eskimos. Captain Roys, soon after his return from the Arctic in the *Superior,* advocated that some sort of facilities be constructed there to aid stranded seamen. When he sailed in *Sheffield* from Cold Spring in 1849, Roys armed her with a large cannon, 4 swivel guns and 24 muskets, solely as a precaution against native attacks.

On at least two occasions Cold Spring ships were threatened by seismic disturbances at sea. In June 1840, the crew of the *Tuscarora* thought they experienced an earthquake shock in the South Pacific. The crew of the *Sheffield,* returning from a four-year whaling voyage in May 1859, excitedly told of an extreme tremor about 300 miles west of Bermuda. They had experienced three shocks, the first of which was the most severe, startling early morning sleepers. Captain H. J. Green said this was the longest, loudest and most severe earthquake of the several he had experienced during his career.

Lookouts stood watch from two to four hours at a time, high aloft in the ship's crows-nest, scanning the horizon for the spout of a whale and other sights of interest. In warmer waters, when hunting for sperms, the seamen stood in open masthead rings, while in colder, polar climes they watched from a canvas shelter, which afforded only scant protection from the cold. Often these men came off watch shivering, eyes tearing, noses blue, and stood, drinking hot chocolate or coffee laced with molasses, while warming themselves around the cook's fire. Seasoned whalemen had little patience with youngsters who could not take it. One sissy of a lad, whom the crewmen teasingly had dubbed the "Pet," complained so much about the cold weather and spent so much time warming up by the galley fire that an officer, in disgust, suggested that next time, "Pet" should stay ". . . at home with Mamma where he can always make good weather of it. . . ."

The whale watch was one of the most boring occupations ever devised. Day after day, mates lamented, "Nothing in sight but water," in their logbooks. Happily, this vacuum was broken by the sight of an occasional ship. Then, the nineteenth century whaleman was fascinated by natural phenomena, for unusual occurrences provided some needed diversion in an otherwise monotonous environment. In their journals and logs the whalers carefully noted every species of fish that they encountered, ranging from the incredible flying fish to great, lethargic sunfish lolling near the surface of temperate and tropic waters. Sharks, accompanied by ubiquitous pilot fish, always present when edible food scraps were tossed overboard, provided drama and action. And somber night watches became tolerable by breath-taking constellations, an occasional glimpse of the Northern Lights, or the much rarer sight of a lunar eclipse or startling comet streaking across the skies.

Old-timers often claimed that they could literally smell a whale, and this might well have been so, for the best grounds were enriched with the oily krill which whales feed upon. On sighting a spouter, the lookout cried, "She Blo-o-o-ws!" And then the wild chase would begin! The Cold Spring whalers either sighted or killed all kinds of cetacea during the course of a voyage, including porpoises, killer whales, blackfish or pilot whales, humpbacks, finbacks, bowheads, blue or sulphur bottoms, sperms, grays, southern rights, and a good number of other species. Some of these, of course, were either too large or too wild to be caught, but were still carefully noted in logs and journals. The whalers pursued anything that could be killed and boiled down into useable oil for illumination or lubrication, or which yielded flexible whalebone which was used in those times for corset stays and in other places where spring steel might be used today.

Peter Dumont, of the *Monmouth,* described the excitement in sighting a whale off the Australian coast in 1855:

> . . . the man at the mast-head sung out in joyful tones the long anticipated watchword of "There she blows! there she blows!"
> The crew below who had been listlessly lounging on deck, or idling on the windlass, sprang to their feet with one accord at this welcome announcement. The captain, who happened to be below at the moment, was immediately summoned by the chief mate, and rushed on deck in an instant to hail the look-out at the mast-head.
> "Hallo! mast-head, there!" echoed his clear distinct voice on the silence.
> "Aye, aye, sir!"
> "Do you see that whale now?"
> "Aye, aye sir!"
> "Where away is he, and what does he look like?"
> "About four points on our larboard bow, sir; he's like a large sperm whale, making right this way, sir."
> "Get the boats ready to lower, men" said the captain, turning to us, "while I go aloft to see what he is."
> [Captain Eldredge] . . . had not been up five minutes before he ordered the boats into the water, and in a twinkling they were all manned and pulling away vigorously in the direction of the whale, which lay like a huge motionless island of rocks in the sea."

Whaleboats, incidentally, were patterned after American Indian canoes, and were among the most fragile, yet trim and perfectly designed craft ever built. Each boat was manned by an officer and five men, including a boatsteerer or harpooner, bow-oarsman, midship-oarsman, tub-oarsman, leading-oar and boatheader. There is an old legend about one Cold Spring crew which consisted of six men, none of whom weighed less than 225 pounds. It included a Kanaka, the heaviest of the lot, who was boatsteerer, Manuel Enos, a huge Portuguese who settled and married in Cold Spring, an Indian from Montauk, Long Island, and several local men: George Barrett, a mate, DeWitt Barrett and William McGarr.

Peter Dumont's narrative continues:

"Get up your harpoons all ready for him," said the captain, as we approached. "Now, lay to your oars, boys, and pull with all your might and main, as though you were pulling for your lives!"

We were fast nearing the whale, and the less the distance became the more excited grew the captain.

"Now, boys, pull! Pull! I tell you! Spring hard, and I'll treat you in the next port we come to!"

Although the men were working with eagerness before, yet this promise seemed to put fresh vigor into their oars, and they shot on with lightning speed.

"Captain, can I dart now? I'm near enough!" cried Nat Scudder, our harpooner.

"I'll tell you when you're near enough," was the reply. "Pull ahead! why don't you pull, boys? There he is, only the ship's length off. Easy, now! he's going to move off; heave up your oars, and take to your paddles; easy now, and quiet! Stand up, Nat, and grab your iron, look out for him, he's right ahead!"

"I see him," cried Nat. "Lay me as close as possible."

"Give it to him," shouted the captain. "Why the Old Neptune don't you dart? Give it to him, I tell you!"

But Nat needed no further urging, for by this time both irons were buried deep in the monster's flesh, and all the sea around was white with his agonized struggles.

"Stern!" exclaimed the captain. "Stern hard, or he will knock our brains out! There, that will do. Now pull in the line—let's haul him up to the boat, and punch him with the lance a little."

It was needless to execute this order, however, for in a second the huge creature shot round and made a straight wake for the boat, apparently bent on crushing us to death in his mad and blind fury. But he missed his object, and threw himself directly across the bows of our boat. The captain, whose keen eye had followed his every motion, sprang to his feet in an instant, and plunged his lance deep into the whale's gigantic side. The monster immediately sank beneath the surface of the water, where he remained for five or ten minutes. During this short reprieve, our men waited with throbbing hearts, watching one another with suspended breath, and in silence.

By this time the boat commanded by the first mate had caught up with us, and lay ready to attack the creature at the first opportunity.

We were not kept waiting long, however, for in a short time he returned to the surface, spouting forth a thick stream of blood and sweeping the water into billows of angry foam. Our captain ordered the chief mate to advance and give him a little more of the harpoon, and immediately the second boat shot forward, and the barbed instrument sunk deep into quivering flesh. A second time the monster plunged beneath the waters, writhing in intolerable agony.

"Now stand to your oars, boys, and be ready to pull stoutly," exclaimed the captain, "for we'll see some stirring sport when he returns, or I'm mistaken."

We waited some fifteen or twenty moments, at the expiration of which time the water again began to boil and foam, and soon after the black bulk of the whale emerged, his tail extended in the air and striking out in every direction, as if bent on revenge for the injuries we had inflicted on him.

He came rapidly onward towards the captain's boat, throwing huge sheets of water on the crew at every sweep of his gigantic tail, and filling it to the very brim.

"Now's your time, Mr. Duval!" shouted the captain, addressing the first mate, "haul upon him, and give him a good dance!"

His orders were obeyed with lightning rapidity, and in a second the mate's boat lay close alongside the monster, its bow touching his back, while Duval was using his lance most skillfully, and making a multitude of swallow-holes through the whale's side.

"Stern me off, boys," cried the mate; in an instant, however, "he's beginning to move again. There he goes—look out for him, for we've got his anger up to the boiling point, now!"

"Spring, men! spring hard for your lives!" shouted the captain, in tones of thunder. "He's coming up to fight!"

The next moment the huge creature came up, writhing in mad rage in the self-same spot where, one minute before, our boat had rocked. His appearance was formidable in the extremest degree, as he rolled from side to side, lashing the sea into a whirlpool of boiling foam, and filling the air with streams of blood from his numerous spout-holes.

The boat of our captain was completely at the mercy of the whale, for it was entirely filled with water, and perfectly useless. The men, however, were quite undismayed at the prospect of a sudden and violent death which seemed to stare them in the face, but sprang vigorously into the water, trusting to the chance of being picked up by the other boats. Before the last man had committed himself to the waves, the whale made a furious attack upon it, taking it in its huge jaws, crushing and shivering it into a thousand pieces. As if completely exhausted by this sudden onslaught, he sunk again under water, and remained submerged for the space of twenty minutes or half an hour. When at length he reappeared on the surface, he exhibited all the outward signs of extreme weariness and weakness; and blood oozed slowly from the multitudiness incisions that covered his body, and life seemed nearly extinct.

With one convulsive effort to retaliate on his enemies, and to regain his failing strength, he rolled over on one side, and threw out his huge fin, but in this effort the faint spark of remaining life went out, and he sank back dead.

Three hearty cheers from our dripping and exhausted ranks broke on the air at this moment, as we began fully to realize that the danger and peril was over, and that our gigantic prize was safe.

"Cut loose, men!" cried the captain, and we proceeded to cut the lines fastened to our harpoons.

The next step was to acquaint the distant ship of our good fortune, which was done by signaling "A dead whale." This signal is made by affixing a good sized piece of black cloth to a pole, which is then stuck into the whale's back. Our black flag, unlike the same sombre-hued pennon when seen on board a pirate ship was hailed with rapture by the crew, and in a few moments the ship had reached us, and taken the dead monster alongside....

This was our first whale adventure, and some among our company, who considered the gain and amusement scarcely equal to the danger and risk of the operation, very openly expressed their hope that it might also be our last, even though we had come safely through the whole affair without loss of life or limb....

Dumont and his companions were fortunate, for the moment, because it was not at all uncommon for a whale, especially an enraged bull sperm or a cow defending her calf, to attack or even destroy a boat, or as on three ominous occasions in the history of American whaling, the whaleship itself. Nathaniel Scudder, who is mentioned in Dumont's narrative, was lost, with the second mate and an entire boat's crew, in 1855, when a whale towed him on a wild Nantucket sleigh ride right into a line of breakers, where the boat capsized and her crew drowned.

Thrashing, mad whales stove in gunwales and smashed numerous boats to matchsticks. Third Mate Weeks of the *Huntsville* was killed by a whale on December 9, 1845. Three, four or more near misses during a voyage were not unusual. Captain Hiram B. Hedges of the *Monmouth* lost an after-oarsman from an upset boat during July 1844, while another Hedges, William, was knocked overboard when a whale which he had harpooned struck the head of his boat. Fortunately he was able to catch hold of the line and the boat crew hauled him in. Another boat from his ship, the *Nathaniel P. Tallmadge,* had its gunwale stove in. The boat was towed back to the ship, the crew keeping her afloat only by cramming clothes into the hole and bailing furiously.

Tragedy struck the *Sheffield* on September 18, 1847, when her waist boat got stove in badly, and one of her men, Scudder Abbot, received compound fractures of the right arm, a broken collar bone and two fractured ribs. The boat had been dashed to pieces, yet in spite of his injuries, Abbot was able to grab hold of a fragment of the craft, and with his good arm, hold on and remain afloat until picked up by another whaleboat. Once aboard the *Sheffield*, his fractures were set, and seemed at first to respond well to medical care. But his condition gradually deteriorated until October 6, when he went into convulsions. Convinced that the end was near, he spoke often of his parents at home, on Main Street in his native Cold Spring. At 11:00 A.M., on October 11, he breathed his last. Then, the following morning, the ship hove to, struck her colors at half-mast, and committed Scudder Abbot to his final resting place. His remains were committed to the deep, as one of his crewmates said, "till the sea shall give up its dead."

If there was sufficient wind the whaleship would come about and pluck the whaleboats from the lonely waters. Often, however, the ships were becalmed and the unlucky boat crews had to row four or five miles, or more, until they reached the mother vessel, some one-to-24 hours later, with their enormous catch in tow. Flares were used for guidance after dark, but it was not uncommon for an exhausted boat crew to spend the night on another whaler, or, at times, ashore with the Siberians or Eskimos.

Once back aboard there was little time to rest or idle. The whale would have to be cut up and "tried" out before predators, such as sharks or orcas, stripped its carcass clean. When the whales were numerous, and easy to catch, there was no time for diversion, with the men catching meals and sleep occasionally and working seven days a week.

During February 1840, while working southeast of the Cape of Good Hope, the crew of the *Tuscarora* endured an especially exhausting three days. It began on February 25, when all hands were called at 6:00 A.M. to make sail and get underway. Soon, the lookout gave the cry and the boats were in the water. One of the crews managed to strike a particularly wild whale, which towed boat and men right out of sight. They were finally able to put the lance to the monster at sunset, and killed him. After a long row back, whale in tow, the boat crew reached sight of *Tuscarora* about 1:00 A.M. The whale was alongside at 2:00 A.M. and the fluke chains were placed around the small near the animal's tail, so that he could not drift away. The chains were secure by 4:00 A.M. and the weary crew was allowed to go below for a few winks of sleep. The "old man" called all hands at 8:00 A.M. and they began to bring the whale aboard. It was cut up and aboard by noon, but then they were not able to start the tryworks because of the cold. The entire day following was spent boiling, or trying, the blubber and putting oil into casks. On the third day the men cleaned and scraped the decks, just in time for the whole cycle to begin once again!

Walter Earle, one of the founders of the Cold Spring Harbor Whaling Museum, and curator for almost 24 years, knew well the procedures for cutting in and trying out, and the following section, describing the whole messy business, is based in substantial part, on his booklet, *How They "'Processed" the Whales*.

First, a section of the bulwark was removed on the starboard side of the ship, between the main and fore masts, leaving an opening of some 10 feet, which was called the gangway. Then the cutting in tackle was rigged on the mainmast, just below the spar of the mainsail (maintop yard); and then the cutting stage, or platform, was lowered below the gangway, with its head to the stern.

The cutting in tackle was a combination of blocks and tackle, with a massive iron bend, called the blubber hook, attached to the fall, or lower, moving block. The whole apparatus was worked by a heavy line which was rove through the sheaves of the blocks and carried forward to the windlass. Every component of this rig was large and heavy, for it had to tear away and hoist on deck the huge chunks of blubber, which weighed a ton or more each, and varied in thickness from 14 inches or more for Arctic whales to 8 inches for animals in warm waters.

The cutting stage consisted of two long planks, which rested on 10 foot booms at each end. The platform was suspended 10 to 12 feet above the water by two blocks through which were rove lines fastened to the ship. The men working on the stage were protected by a handrail and by "monkey ropes" tied to their waists.

Next, a boatsteerer was sent down on the whale in a sling, or monkey rope. Using a sharp, chisel-like knife, called the spade, he cut a hole through the blubber between the whale's left eye and flipper, to receive the blubber hook. He cut a deep gash, called the scarf, in a semicircle above and around the hole, and then the blubber hook was put through, always with great difficulty. By this time, two mates, or the captain and a mate, had gone down on the stage. Equipped with long-handled spades, measuring 12 feet or more, they cut down through the blubber, from each end of the scarf, in a spiral pattern. As they cut, the men at the windlass—six or eight of them—strained at their labors, slowly working the blubber away from the flesh and pulling it upward until the tackle was two-blocked, or as tight as it could go.

At this point, a mate on deck would cut out a second hole through the blanket piece, a few feet above the deck, and then set a second hook into that hole. When the second line was hove taut, the mate took a boarding knife, which resembled a long handled sword, and used it to slice off the strip above the second hook. The first blanket piece was then swung across the deck, careening the ship violently with its sheer weight. This was an extremely dangerous operation, and several members of a Sag Harbor crew were crushed to death by a falling blanket piece. The piece was then lowered through the main hatch into the blubber room, where three or four men took charge of it. They cut it into smaller "horse" pieces, which were piled between decks for the moment. The blubber room was a foul smelling hole, littered with gore and blood as deep as boot tops.

The cutting in continued until the blubber was stripped down to the tail flukes. As it was being stripped, the whale revolved slowly, the blubber unwinding like an apple paring cut in a single peel. The head was cut off during the stripping. If a sperm, it was taken aft and hung on the side of the ship for attention later; and if a baleen, it was cut through horizontally, and the upper portion, containing the "whalebone," was hoisted on the deck. The lower part was consigned to the deep for the predators.

The moment the whale was cut its blood gushed out, and in a few minutes the water around the cutting stage was churning with vicious sharks, slashing and tearing at the whale. Every now and then the men on the stage, unable to hold back their contempt for the creatures, would thrust a blade into the belly of a shark, adding more gore, guts and turmoil to an already dreadful scene.

A fire had been lighted under the pots in the tryworks, which would be used to boil out the oil. Usually, the works for each voyage were built on deck during the early weeks of the trip when the men had nothing much to do. The works consisted of a brick furnace containing two or three huge iron trypots, with grates beneath them and fire doors in front above the grates. The pots varied from 120 to 200 gallons in capacity. Usually, a heavy, saucerlike iron tank for water was set in under the grates to prevent the deck from being charred, while a platform was built above the works as protection against rain and snow and to support the copper chimneys running up from the furnace. Smaller ships generally had no platform above the works or chimney to carry the smoke away. The fires in the works were started with wood, but as soon as some of the blubber had been tried out the pieces of skin attached to it were used for fuel. These strips, called cracklings, produced an intense heat, as well as heavy black smoke.

If the catch was a sperm whale, the spermaceti was bailed out of the head "case," and immediately put into the trypots and boiled down. Spermaceti is a waxy, viscous, semifluid substance, which produced top quality oil. Then, the lower jaw was severed and put aside for the teeth and skeletal bone, called panbone, which would be used by the men to make scrimshaw; while the third part, the "junk," was cut up and boiled. If the head was from a baleen whale, the bone was sliced off, trimmed and stacked on deck, but only after everything else had been done.

The horse pieces were brought up on deck from the blubber room, and were then reduced to still smaller pieces called books or bibles. The pages were formed by making thin slices, which were bound by skin, so that the piece resembled a book in appearance. The cutting was done with a razor-sharp drawshave knife, called a mincing knife. The object of paging, of course, was to present a greater surface for faster boiling. The bibles were put into the pots and boiled continuously until used up.

Old-time sailors said that you could smell a whaler boiling twenty miles off. The process, incidentally, was tricky. Great care was required to make certain that the oil did not burn or discolor, or that the blubber did not become stale or rancid before boiling. A man with a long handled skimmer scooped off the cracklings as they rose to the top, while others ladled out the boiling oil into cooler pots. As the oil cooled, it was poured into huge casks, which had been set up —from shooks, heads and hoops stored below—by the cooper, who then bunged them before they were lowered into the holds to be stored. Sometimes, while the oil was boiling, the cook would take sweet dough and make doughnuts which, believe-it-or-not, were fried right in the trypots!

Finally, after five or six hours of the hardest, dirtiest, and most disagreeable work a seaman could ever know, clean up time came, with a task still harder and dirtier. By now the whole ship was covered with a heavy, black, oily film. The deck was slippery with oil and gore and the men's clothes were saturated with the stuff. The sailors, exhausted but encouraged with their prize, began to scour the decks, scrape down the tryworks and refit the boats for another day's whaling.

While they were cleaning up some men scraped, washed and cleaned part of the flesh, krill and organic residue from the whalebone. If possible, it was then left in the open to dry until it would no longer "answer," or smell. When no longer green, the dried bone was neatly tied with spunyarn into bundles of about a hundred. pounds each and stowed below in a dry place. Before reaching port the ship's name was lettered on a piece of pine which was fastened to the butt end of each bundle to be shipped to market. The oil also required some care, lest it spoil or the casks leak. During the voyage home the oil was frequently checked, with the casks being watered down to keep them tight, and leaky ones being recoopered.

More often than not the whaler was met with disappointment, for few of the whales he sighted ever ended up in the trypot. The percentage of animals spotted and pursued, in comparison to those which were actually taken, was relatively small, and approached, perhaps, only 10 to 20 percent at the most. For example, from April through July, 1849, the crew of the *Nathaniel P. Tallmadge* sighted over 84 whales, yet only a few ever reached the trypots.

Many leviathans were lost after they had been harpooned. Large or wild whales could tow a boat for 12 hours or more, without tiring, or would foul the lines, forcing the mate to cut the line in desperation— or fright. At other times an animal would be lost because the iron either broke or "drawed" out. When one got away, the old whalemen used to say that he "turned flukes" or "turned tail."

Not all whales float when dead. Sperms remain just awash, while some others sink. As a result, many baleen whales were lost before they could be towed back to the ship. Other times, when a whale was especially wild, the boat crew would bend on a drogue, which was a block of wood or a heavy, oak tub, which was used to check the mammal's speed through the water. Some still managed to outrun their pursuers, only to die elsewhere. Another whaleship might chance to spot one of these drift whales, and when they did there was much rejoicing among the crew, for half of the work of taking and killing the whale had already been done for them!

Sometimes they would kill a whale and get him alongside, only to discover in disappointment, that he was a "dry skin," or a sick whale so poor in oil that it was not worth saving. Even animals which had been "swept and fluked," or secured to the ship's side were not completely safe. During very rough weather, a large whale could break its chains and drift off, unnoticed during the night.

Occasionally, a whale was found with a harpoon or two, tokens of previous battle with other whaleboats, still imbedded in its blubber. The crew of the *Sheffield* once took such a whale, which had two harpoons in it and three drogues still attached to the trailing lines. But one of the most interesting—and amazing—findings of another ship's harpoon involved another Cold Spring ship.

In 1908 the whaleship *Andrew Hicks,* Captain C. S. Church, returned to New Bedford, Massachusetts, where she had cleared in 1884 to sail on 22 subsequent voyages from San Francisco. With her, upon returning, was a harpoon which had been darted by a boatsteerer of the Cold Spring bark *Alice* many years before, and which the crew of the *Andrew Hicks* had found imbedded in a whale during one of her cruises to the North Pacific. The iron had broken off in the animal and evidently had lodged in a moveable joint, for a groove was worn in the shank through the action of the head rubbing against it.

The harpoon, incidentally, was identified by the name *"Alice"* stippled into the toggle head. Ever since whaling had become an industry it had been the custom for each whaling firm to have the name of its vessels stamped into every harpoon. This facilitated identification when two or more boats of different ships were operating in the same waters. If the whale got away and was later found dead, the harpoons would quickly reveal which of the boats had killed it.

Cold Spring whalers were often innovators and attempted to use the latest whaling gear whenever possible. A bomb lance, perfected by C. C. Brand of Norwich, Connecticut, in 1852, came to the attention of Captain Thomas Roys, of the *Sheffield,* just about two years later. In 1854, he carefully described the new invention:

> ...there is a bomb lance fired from the shoulder enclosing a steel head with a half Pound of Powder which has been used this Season by the Ship Daniel Wood with Success to kill Whales it explodes in the whale tearing his Joints from the sockets and producing quick death.

This device, of course, was used instead of a lance to kill whales; it did not fire the harpoon.

THE *TUSCARORA*
Sailed from Cold Spring Harbor 1837-1851

THE *SPLENDID*
Sailed from Cold Spring Harbor 1844-1860

THE *SHEFFIELD*
Sailed from Cold Spring Harbor 1845-1859

THE *RICHMOND*
Sailed from Cold Spring Harbor 1843-1849

THE *NATHANIEL P. TALLMADGE*
Sailed from Cold Spring Harbor 1843-1855

THE BARK *MONMOUTH*
Sailed from Cold Spring Harbor 1836-1862

THE *EDGAR*
Sailed from Cold Spring Harbor 1852-1855

THE *HUNTSVILLE*
Sailed from Cold Spring Harbor 1844-1858

In November 1852 Captain Freeman H. Smith, writing from Lahaina, Hawaii, presented an idea to the owners of the *Huntsville,* which at that time, although not unique, was quite perceptive. He asked John H. and Walter Restored Jones' permission to buy a schooner of about 100 tons, to be used as a tender for his ship. Smith planned to use the smaller vessel in the Gulf of Penzhinskaya in the Okhotsk Sea, where he had seen plenty of Russian whales during a previous cruise. There was a problem, though, in working there, because there was a swift current and a smooth, slatey bottom, which made it very dangerous to lay at anchor. There was, however, a safe anchorage about 50 miles away from ". . . as Good whaling Ground as I ever saw. . . ."

In referring to the past season, Smith explained that ". . . the Only reason i hav not filled my ship is becaus i did not have a . . . tender. There is no one foolishly head strong Enough to trust his Ship and Company in this place where there is no safe anchorage. . . . But a Schooner it is different for We could Lay off and in any kind of weather. . . ."

Captain Smith estimated that the project would cost between $3,000 and $5,000, and that he could provision the vessel from his own ship. He believed that he could fill both the schooner and the ship in just one season.

The owners replied, in the affirmative, but with certain reservations. First, they wanted Captain Smith to ship home all of the oil he had on board so that he could fill up completely. He could indeed buy the schooner, provided that he could sell it again, for approximately the same price he had paid for it. Smith was authorized to buy the tender, and was to use good judgement in the purchase, ". . . not to allow fancy or fashion to govern you."

Unfortunately, there are no records available which indicate whether Captain Smith actually put this plan into action. It is known that he did, however, sail from Honolulu on March 28, 1853, for the Okhotsk Sea. A ship spoke to *Huntsville* there, and she had taken 10 whales by July 24. She returned to Honolulu on October 24, and while not filled to capacity, had a respectable catch, resulting in 150 barrels of sperm whale oil, 2,700 barrels of whale oil and 30,000 pounds of bone. It was a good season's catch by anyone's standards!

6

The Whaler's Lot

... My young lads i will tell you that you must pull your Selves about when you are on board of a ship you must work hard all day and when night comes you must Stand a watch and then Sleep when you can ...
C. A. Babcock, *Tuscarora,* 1839

WHEN NOT chasing spouters, the lives of Cold Spring whalers were filled with monotony, keeping the captains and mates at wits' ends trying to create busy work, all of which surely was displeasing to the crews. "Humbugging" they called it, and this labor usually consisted of tarring and tending the rigging, patching and mending sails and canvaswork, preparing spunyarn, and making deck swabs, wipers, bungs, pennants for the mast tops and, on occasion, even shoes for the ship's Kanakas.

Anyone who has ever sailed knows that there is continual maintenance and upkeep aboard ship. On a whaler the decks, holds, passageways and staterooms, as well as the hull—inside and out—had to be washed down to rid the ship of foul smelling residue remaining from the cutting in process. This was also a good time to get everything shipshape again and stowed in proper places.. On calm days at sea the ships were painted inside and out and if the winds permitted, even the masts, yards and bowsprit might be done. On a return voyage, while passing not far off Bermuda, the crew of the *Alice* had just finished painting the boats and had turned them over to dry. Suddenly, at 6:00 P.M., there was a cry from the masthead: a gam of sperms—some small cows and two calves! Ignoring the fresh paint, the boats were lowered in a wink. It was worth the inconvenience for the larboard crew took one of the prizes, which was safely alongside by 5:00 the next morning.

While the crew was humbugging, the ships' specialists were hard at work. The cooper made buckets, buoys and drogues. He took this opportunity to set up oil casks and repair damaged barrels and casks. He also assisted the carpenter in dressing hundreds of poles which would be needed for mounting the ship's whalecraft. The carpenter, working from the large inventory of planks on deck, built platforms and watch shacks, but spent most of his time repairing damage to the hull, boats and rigging. A few ships carried blacksmiths, who spent hours at the grindstone, honing harpoons, lances and spades.

While some more principled captains permitted no work on Sundays, including lowering the boats and pursuing whales, most took little or no cognizance of the Sabbath. Christmas, as well as most other holidays, meant little difference in the whalers' routine, save for, perhaps, a special meal of fresh meat or fish. Most of the crews could claim just a few minutes or hours for their own. Isaac Jessup, a harpooner aboard *Sheffield,* wrote in his journal that "Sunday . . . I believe . . . is allowed on board most ships. . . . there is no Sunday off soundings [at sea] at least I was told so a few minutes ago by one who has followed the sea many years."

When fortunate enough to "knock off" on a Sunday or holiday, the crew prayed from Bibles or psalm books or reread old newspapers, magazines, books and letters from home. And perhaps they would "line their insides" with a good dinner, then read some more, lounge on deck if the weather was pleasant, or just lie in their bunks. Meanwhile, others tended to personal tasks, such as trimming hair, beards and mustaches, washing and mending clothes. Lonely sailors wrote letters back home. Some would while the time playing checkers and cards, or pitching peas for amusement or profit.

Every whaleman loved to "gam" or visit with his contemporaries. When it was very calm, two or more whaleships would heave to and lower boats, allowing the crews to visit other ships, mingle and swap sea stories, tell tall tales, compare professional notes, or just sing songs, from early morning to 10:00 or 11:00 o'clock at night. ". . . heard news that the ship *Alex Mansfield* had ben condemnd in Otehite [Tahiti] and Douglass has now got the *France* of Sagharbor and John Howell has ben kild by a Spurm Whale and the Ship *Pocahontas* foundered and her Crew was picked up on their way to the Bay of islands. . . ." And so they exchanged the news of the day. Gams, apart from social considerations, also meant fresh food, tobacco, and the like which were bartered liberally between the ships.

Whalers had to provide their own entertainment thousands of miles from civilization, so no gam was complete without an old-fashioned sing-a-long. There were ballads of the sea and of love, sad and happy songs, and most favorite of all, songs of home. Three of these chanties, which were sung on a Cold Spring ship, survive. Each had been recorded by Charles Babcock during his 1839-1841 voyage in *Tuscarora,* and were, no doubt, his favorites. First, there is "Gaily the Troubadour," a song of a lady's longing for her returning Crusader:

> Gaily the troubadour touched his guitar
> When he was hastening home from the war
> Singing "Palestine hither I come
> Lady love, lady love, welcome me home"

And then "A Soldier's Gratitude," a ballad of a man's thoughts of home:

> Whatever my fate where e'r I roam
>   By sorrow still oppressed
> I'll ne'er forget the peaceful home
>   That gave a wand'rer rest . . .
> Still may you claim a Soldier's thanks
>   A Soldier's gratitude

Lastly, "Loss of the *Albion*" a chantey of a shipwreck which claimed 50 souls in 1822—a song of the sea if there ever was one:

> Come all you jovial Sailor boys
>   And listen unto me
> A dreadful story I will tell
>   Which happened on the Sea
> The loss of the *Albion* Ship my boys
>   Upon the Irish Coast
> Where most of her crew and passengers
>   Were all completely lost. . . .

Hobbies and crafts flourished among whalemen. Ship models were the rage during 1849 in the *Sheffield*. Other sailors collected seashells and fashioned them into trinkets or wove mats for folks back home. But scrimshaw was the whalers' own folk art, and Cold Spring men were active practitioners. They called it "scrimshontering" or "scrimshantering." While the origin of the word is hazy, it appears to have been derived from the Dutch word *Skrimshander,* meaning a fellow who is lazy or lounges around too much. The Cold Spring whalers cut buggy whips from black baleen and carved canes from the white panbone of sperm whales. Some examples of scrimshaw, especially those which were scratched on highly polished sperm whale teeth, with the lines filled with tobacco juice, lamp black, soot, ashes or India ink, were truly works of art.

Every captain had to keep an official ship's log, which was generally filled with dull, terse entries relating to the weather, ship's course or working of the sails. But many of the literate mates, and even a few of the seamen, kept private journals in which they entered their own personal feelings and thoughts of the many interesting happenings which occurred during a particular voyage. At the time the journals were written there was little pleasure in recording a day's events —by the light of a swaying whale oil lamp—late at night after an exhausting day on deck. In rough weather an ink bottle could spill and spoil an entire page of entries, and on one humorous occasion a ship's pet dog trotted—with dirty paws—right across a tired whaleman's page. Many of the ships, incidentally, carried mascots, including dogs, cats and even a parrot or two.

Not all of the whalemen were interested in intellectual or artistic pursuits. Some were avid sportsmen and enjoyed swimming—when the sharks were not too curious—sailing in the whaleboats and clamming and fishing. One popular, yet sadistic, sport involved chasing sharks in the whaleboats, harpooning them, and then hauling the creatures up on deck, where each man had his turn at attacking the hated fish with anything at hand.

Sickness or accident were, perhaps, the greatest fears of the whalemen, aside from shipwreck or injury by a whale. Medical care, at the most, was rudimentary. The captain, mate, or perhaps a seaman who had a little medical knowledge would serve as best he could as the ship's doctor. No voyage was without some sort of sickness, whether contracted in the islands or some dirty port which the ships had visited. Sanitary conditions aboard the whaleships were generally lacking, and practically every vessel harbored rats and cockroaches, which periodically had to be smoked out.

It was not unusual at all for the majority of the crew, a mate, the cook, or even the captain himself to be confined to their bunks with some sort of malady. Captain Edward Halsey of the *Monmouth* took deathly ill with apparent dysentary while at sea in 1846. He put into Cape Town immediately, fearful for his life, but soon recuperated.

Halsey's values fluctuated, for about six years previous, when in command of the *Tuscarora,* he had refused even to take note of four or five sick crewmen.

Poor diets, heavy in carbohydrates and sparse in protein were substantially lacking in vitamin C foods, such as fresh fruit and vegetables. This, of course, contributed to scurvy, the most feared disease of the whaler. Often two or three men came down with it during a voyage. Hopefully, they would reach a hospital before the illness had time to take its ravaging toll. Writing from the Cape of Good Hope in December 1846, Captain Edward Halsey lamented that three or four of his men had scurvy. Halsey felt that it was the result of their potatoes having rotted during the first two weeks at sea, leaving the crew without a valuable source of vitamin C.

Aside from colds, toothaches were probably the most common shipboard ailment. Sailors often complained of sleepless nights, suffering from a diseased molar and perhaps an aching ear. There was no relief until the captain extracted the painful culprit. A number of diseases were common to the whaleships. Consumption or tuberculosis was hastened no doubt by poor air circulation in the steerage areas below deck. Several men, including a Chilean named Joseph Hidalgo and Kanaka Charles of the *Alice,* lost their lives to tuberculosis. Another Kanaka, Tom, who sailed on the same 1854-1858 voyage, died of apparent dropsy or edema. Contaminated water caused dysentary, a malady quite common among whalers. Isaac Jessup, writing of a terrific bout he experienced aboard *Sheffield,* noted that an ". . . attack of dysentary commencing this morning weakened me so much that I could [not] walk the length of the deck. When night came I believe it the sickest day I can remember of having ever. . . ." It appears Jessup actually had a severe case of food poisoning, for he recovered quickly. Many fevers, as well as a variety of social diseases, were contracted in the numerous islands and strange ports which the ships visited. The crew of the *Huntsville* was overjoyed when they narrowly averted a smallpox epidemic at Guam in 1856, clearing port just as the disease broke out. Fortunately no one aboard the ship had been exposed to it.

Captain Roys of the *Sheffield* was less fortunate. Arriving off Honolulu in September 1853 with a good cargo of whale oil from the Arctic, he learned that there was an outbreak of smallpox in the port. Wisely, he decided not to bring the ship in, instead going ashore alone for the night. As Providence would have it, a week later Roys was stricken

THE WHALER'S LOT 57

with the pox. As soon as he realized what was the matter the captain refused to permit anyone into his cabin, except the steward, who fortunately had had the disease previously and was immune. Roys remained in this isolation for four weeks and through his good sense no one else aboard the ship was afflicted.

Crushed hands and feet, twisted wrists and ankles, broken bones, split thumbs and cuts from the sharp whalecraft were quite common, with rough weather, weakened health and generally dangerous working conditions all being contributing factors. Then there is always the pervading conclusion, considering the character of some of the men who signed on, that some "accidents" were actually deliberate assaults.

No reason to dwell on the sinister—Cold Spring ships were noted for their heroes. On board *Sheffield,* in the late fall of 1849, a seaman named John Culver was reefing the topsails, when the canvas suddenly struck his head causing him to faint and almost fall to the deck below. It would have been certain death if another man, known as "Long Jack," had not risked his own life by grabbing Culver and pulling him to safety into the masttop. The next day Isaac Jessup, while working the fore spencer sail from the lee to weather side, lost his foothold on the main stay and fell to the deck. Jessup's head struck hard enough to stun him. A mate helped the harpooner up and took him to the master's cabin where Captain Roys cut off some hair around the cut and applied an adhesive plaster. The wound did not prove any too serious, but a sore head and a lame knee kept Jessup confined to his bunk for a day or so.

On October 30, 1843, James F. Barnet, a bright young cabin boy on the *Nathaniel P. Tallmadge,* was discovered missing when all hands were called to make sail. They found no trace of him after a thorough search, save for the clothes he wore, which were laying on his sea chest. Further investigation revealed that the quarter watch had seen James come on deck during the night, about 12:30 A.M., and then go into the mizzen chains. They thought nothing strange of it, and since they were aft and heard nothing, surmised that the boy went below again and was there until the watch was called in the morning. James had suffered several fainting spells previous to his disappearance, so it was presumed that the lad had suffered another and fallen overboard.

Sometimes shipboard routine was disrupted by outbursts of irrational behavior or violent fits by crewmen suffering from mental instability, fever, or, perhaps, epilepsy. Remember, these crews were not screened, and hard-pressed captains would sign on practically anyone to fill a billet. Many of these men had never seen a doctor in their lives, and could have been afflicted by all manner of mental illnesses. A Kanaka from the Kings Mills Group, thought to have been deranged, lowered one of the *Nathaniel P. Tallmadge's* boats, rowed two miles astern and disappeared. The means the captains used to deal with abnormal behavior were usually harsh. Captain George Penney of the *Alice,* for example, clapped one disturbed man into irons and kept him there for several days until he "came to his senses."

In his capacity as the ship's doctor, the captain also was somewhat of a pharmacist, prescribing medicines and cures for whatever ailed his men. His methods were primitive—to say the least—as Captain Eli White's treatment of an injured man attests. While taking in sail aboard the *Sheffield,* at sunset in May 1846, Scudder Abbot fell from the topsail yard to the deck. The mates picked him up unconscious, blood streaming from his mouth and nose, and brought him aft. Captain White immediately *bled* the poor man, following the belief that bleeding helped relieve sickness and injury. Abbot was then undressed and laid in his berth, his shipmates fearing that he would die there. But somehow he pulled through the night, and with a slow recovery and five and a half weeks of rest, returned to duty.

Every American ship, as far back as 1790, was required by law to carry a medicine chest. Most of them were put up by a seaport apothecary, and the remedies were keyed to a book of directions by either numbers or letters so that the user could easily diagnose symptoms and administer one or more preparations to treat a specific sickness. These drugs and medicines were generally the best available at the time for emergency treatment. They were all fairly essential to keeping the crew alive and working. Naturally, a whaleman's account was charged with any medicine he consumed!

Quite often even a seriously ill man would respond well to such medication, and if he was lucky enough to be near a civilized port, and the captain humane and willing, the whaleman might hope to receive further attention from a doctor or a hospital. Not everyone was so fortunate, however, for whaling captains were not noted for sympathy when it would mean losing a portion of a season to bring a sick man back to port. Either the man pulled through and got better, or he died and was buried at sea while the captain reverently read from scripture.

Cold Spring ships, being no better nor worse than any others in the fishery, had their full share of insubordination and mutiny. Long, dreary periods at sea tended to magnify petty differences, causing officer-crew relationships to deteriorate and morale, in general, to ebb with each passing week. It was difficult, for even very short expanses of time, to maintain discipline among the type of men who sailed in whaling ships, and a captain or mate who happened to be particularly unreasonable or rough might expect a good ration of trouble. Few officers were universally liked, or even tolerated, by their crews. Personal journals are filled with bitter and sometimes obscene regard for superiors. In February 1840, when the "old man" would not take *Tuscarora* into the Cape of Good Hope for fresh food, the crew became very agitated. One man privately cursed Captain Halsey, hoping that he would be ". . . the first one Sick with the Scervy. . . ." Later he thought Halsey a damn fool—and worse—for the way in which he ran the ship.

Bare knuckle justice, whether openly enforced by the captain or surreptitiously administered behind the deck house by the mates, was the common law aboard whaleships. Captain White clapped two of the *Sheffield*'s men into irons for four days for attempting to desert and refusing duty. Flogging was a generally accepted method of breaking an especially ornery seaman. While the *Monmouth* was anchored at the Marias Islands, off the west coast of Mexico, Captain Hedges called the crew aft at 7:00 one morning. David Kilyas had abused the second mate, so he was seized up in the rigging and flogged with a cat-o'-nine-tails before the entire crew. Whalers' justice was brutal and quick, yet usually effective. Somehow these men, who had been placed in irons or flogged or cuffed by the captain or mates, either contained their hatred and anguish, or they would have to resort to mutiny or desertion in the next port.

Captain Roys, of the *Sheffield,* who had a brilliant reputation as a whaleman, experienced a full-blown mutiny in February 1850. The trouble originally began at Valparaiso, Chile, back in December when a number of the crew refused duty because it was Sunday. Mr. Green, the mate, gave them time to reconsider, but when twelve still would not cooperate he had them placed in irons and taken below. Some of the men decided to work, so their irons were removed and they returned to duty. Captain Roys was furious with the remaining men. He had them taken aft and mustered all hands to witness punishment. There, Roys administered one of the most severe examples of flogging ever endured aboard a Cold Spring whaler. John Dalton, probably the ringleader, received a brutal twenty-six lashes; Henry Smith got nineteen; while John O'Brien, Richard O'Maley and Daniel B. Rash each received seventeen; with eleven to James McGann and ten to John McDermot. After Captain Roys had spent his wrath on the malcontents, he sent them forward to their bunks to tend their wounds and recuperate. Make no mistake—despite Roys' merciless handling of this incident—he could be fair and clement in handling his crews.

But trouble was only beginning to brew. The rebellious crew members began to threaten and vow vengeance both in public and in private. Some began to suspect that there was a deep and diabolical conspiracy. On February 8, 1850, grasping the tension in the air, Roys had the blacksmith's forge dismantled and replaced it with a brig for the seven men who had been flogged. By that afternoon, with their place of confinement completed, the men were put in irons and locked up until the ship reached California. One of the more mutinous prisoners angrily boasted that he could break his bonds, but Captain Roys was not ready to let him keep his pledge, so he had the man placed in another pair of irons which was so strong that it could "resist the strength of ten men." This man, incidentally, was considered to have been especially dangerous since he had threatened to murder someone within the month.

After questioning the crew, the captain was shocked to learn that the seven attempted mutineers had planned to kill the officers and crew, take charge of the ship, then run her ashore near the gold fields, where they would set her afire and escape. If the plot had not been discovered they probably would have murdered all who displeased them, for they had previously threatened ". . . to string some [of the officers and crewmen] to the yard arm & drink the heart's blood of others. . . ."

As soon as *Sheffield* arrived at San Francisco, Captain Roys boarded the U.S.S. *Warren* and convinced the captain to take the prisoners into custody. The Navy captain quickly agreed, but admonished Roys for having been too lenient with the rebels. Perhaps, he added, Roys should have left them on some barren island, saving everyone any further inconvenience!

There was one Cold Spring mutiny which ranks among the most bizarre in the annals of whaling. It occurred during the 1848 voyage of the *Tuscarora,* and first came to the attention of her owners in May 1851 when the New Bedford whaler *Rodman* returned home with the first reports of a unique double mutiny. On January 29, 1851, just as the *Rodman* touched at Aitutaki, Cook Islands, in the South Pacific, a boat bearing nine men arrived at the island. The sailors claimed to have abandoned the *Tuscarora,* with the rest of the crew taking two other boats, some ninety miles south of Mangaia Island, which lies in the same group.

Captain William Allyn was very shorthanded, so he asked the men if they would ship on for the *Rodman*'s return voyage home. One man agreed, but the rest refused and would have remained on Aitutaki if the natives had not intimated that they would not be welcome there. They then agreed to sail with Captain Allyn only with the understanding that he would try to land them at Rarotonga, which is also in the same group. If they could not make that island, the strangers agreed to go home in the *Rodman,* but only as a last resort. So, their boat was taken aboard and Captain Allyn set a course for Rarotonga.

When it appeared that he could not reach Rarotonga, Captain Allyn decided that he would have to take the men home with him, even though they were very mutinous and insolent. When he told them his plan, the men became openly insubordinate and went below. After consulting among themselves, the rascals returned to the deck armed with knives and, declaring that they would not work, they retreated to the fo'c's'le. Seeing that these men were on the verge of taking his ship, and worrying that some of his own crew might join them, the captain changed course and immediately made for Rarotonga. When he figured that the ship was about thirty miles away from the island, he launched the mutineers' boat, gave them provisions for a fortnight, and then took the wise precaution of ordering his own crew below. Heading straight for the fo'c's'le gangway, Allyn told the men that he was giving them an opportunity to reach Rarotonga if they still wanted to. They agreed, so he called each man up, one by one, and put him into the boat.

Oddly enough, one of the men volunteered to return in the *Rodman,* and during the long voyage home revealed the true circumstances of the entire affair. It seems that the *Tuscarora* had been scuttled by some of the departed men, who had drilled several large augur holes through her bows. He did mention privately that they had taken the boat with the captain's permission. He would say no more, and it was several weeks after the *Rodman*'s return before the full story became known. It was then learned that Captain Samuel Leek touched with the *Tuscarora* at Mangaia in late December for recruits, some five weeks out of Honolulu. On December 24, just as the ship was clearing port, nine men refused duty, proposing that Captain Leek give them a boat so that they could return to the island. Since they were very surly, the captain agreed, somewhat reluctantly.

When she cleared Mangaia, *Tuscarora* was leaking thousands of pump strokes per day because of the holes which the mutineers had bored in her bows. Finally, the leaks were checked, but not fully, for she still took on about 700 strokes per hour when she arrived at Rarotonga on December 25. Realizing that he would have to heave out for repairs, Captain Leek set a course for Sydney, Australia, which lay some 3,000 miles away. *Tuscarora* arrived there on January 24, 29 months out, with 2,100 barrels of whale oil. Soon afterward, Captain Leek was told that her repairs would cost more than the value of the ship, because of her age and the extent of the leaks. She was condemned in March and sold to Robert Towns, a local shipowner, for $7,500.

Bobbie Towns was a shrewd former sea captain who had come ashore in 1842 and started a sperm whaling fleet out of Sydney in 1847. Somehow he refitted *Tuscarora* for sea again and she sailed on December 4, 1851, under a Captain Smith for the South Seas whale grounds. *Tuscarora*'s career under Towns' flag was short-lived, for by the late 1850s the majority of his ships were laid up at "Rotten Row," a graveyard of old ships at Sydney.

By today's standards, there was one crew disturbance aboard a Cold Spring ship which was more of a labor dispute than an act of insubordination. It happened in February 1857, when the New London whaling bark *Hannah Brewer* returned from cruising around Kerguelen, the "Island of Desolation," and was condemned at St. Helena. Captain Jerimiah Eldredge of the *Monmouth*, who happened to be in port, decided to take on the *Hannah Brewer*'s 115 barrels of oil for freight. But this would not be as easy as he thought, for his officers and crew, apparently to a man, refused to haul the oil in unless they were paid for their extra labors.

Wisely, Captain Eldredge persuaded the entire group to appear with him for arbitration before the United States Vice-Commercial Agent for St. Helena. The captain said that he was willing to bargain, offering the men three shillings per day—the prevailing wage for laborers at the island. Half of the men rejected the offer and demanded at least five shillings. One man objected to the seaworthiness of the ship, which he claimed leaked badly in rough weather and had pumps which were in very poor condition. He felt that the addition of the *Hannah Brewer*'s oil might place the ship in further danger. The chief mate readily agreed and produced the ship's log, which revealed that *Monmouth* had been leaking badly for some time.

The Commercial Agent tried in vain to reason with the men, using every argument and influence he possessed to convince them to haul the oil aboard. He pointed out, at Captain Eldredge's request, that they might be paid out of the freight charges in the same proportion as their lays, but this, too, was futile. After a delay of several hours, unable to get his own men to cooperate, Eldredge paid part of the crew of the *Hannah Brewer* to hoist the oil on board.

The art of navigation was somewhat primitive aboard whaleships, and many times the crew, and possibly the captain himself, were genuinely surprised to raise a particular port on the first try. The captain, as well as the several mates, performed the actual mechanics of navigation and piloting. Of course, every ship had a compass to hold a course by, a spyglass for piloting and usually a barometer to give some advance indication of an approaching typhoon or hurricane. By determining the sun angle from sextant sights and making computations, with the aid of fairly accurate time from the ship's chronometer, the whalers were able to determine their position.

When the whaler was filled with oil and bone, or the season over, the captain would return to port so that his crew could relax and he could repair and recruit the ship. In the Atlantic, St. Helena, Tristan da Cuhna and Cape Town were popular ports of call after long cruises on the South Atlantic or sub-Antarctic grounds. In the Pacific, Honolulu was a favorite of the Cold Spring whalers, but the following ports, in order of frequency of visits, were also popular: Lahaina, Hawaii; Hobart, Tasmania; Sydney, Australia; Guam; Tahiti; Bay of Islands, New Zealand; as well as a host of other ports and islands throughout the south and western Pacific.

There were two seasons out of Hawaii, the summer, on the Arctic grounds, and the winter, in the South Seas. Crew turnover was very high and often reached three times—or more—during the course of a three or four year voyage. In fact, every time a ship put into port between seasons as many as twenty men were either paid off and discharged, or deserted. Those who shipped over for a better lay, or stayed for the same rate, usually received a small advance, but wisely only after the oil and bone were offloaded, fresh stores hauled aboard and repairs to the ship completed. Some captains, especially when calling at a port during the midseason, feared that their crews would run off if they advanced them any money. There was no more pitiful whine than that of a penniless sailor in a good liberty port!

Peter Dumont of the *Monmouth* wrote a vivid description of the typical sailor's liberty after a number of months on the "grounds:"

> A whaleman who has been away from home some six or eight months is a singular-looking object, as one may easily infer. . . . His shirt, jacket and trowsers are diversified with innumerable patches, of all sizes, shapes and colors, which are sewed on with his own clumsy fingers, more used to the lance and harpoon than to the needle, and consequently present rather a "journeyman" appearance. His garments are literally a coat of many colors, as well as many materials, and thus accoutred, with a pipe in his mouth, he is ready to meet anything on the face of the earth, whether it be whale or whirlwind.
>
> But the whaleman in port, after he has had time to renovate himself both outwardly and inwardly is altogether a different personage. You may see him emerging from the tempting portals of "The Sailor's Home" in an indescribable state of jollity and good humor with himself and all the rest of the world. His sympathies are readily awakened towards the most glaringly improbable tale of want or suffering, and he scatters his money right and left, with prodigal plenty, until some morning he wakes to find his pockets unfurnished, and his inseparable companion, the black bottle, empty, and he is obliged to fall back on the unfailing resource—another long whaling voyage.

Not all of the crewmen were as irresponsible as Dumont would have us believe. Some of them were sober gentlemen who regularly attended church whenever they had the opportunity. Missionaries had settled throughout the Pacific during the nineteenth century, so that practically every settlement, large or small, had a church or meeting house, which on the Sabbath was filled with natives, traders and whalers.

It was hard work finishing out one season and preparing for another. The oil and bone were usually offloaded, and if the local going price was satisfactory it was sold on the spot, and if not, the "takings" were either shipped home in another whaleship or merchantman as freight, or consigned as far as London if the market there was right.

There were generally three major expenses in port: paying off the crew, recruiting and repairing the ship. Honolulu, in spite of its immense popularity with captains and crews alike, was the most expensive port in the Pacific. It usually cost from $3,000 to $6,000 to repair and refit a vessel for another season. Caulking the hulls and repairing the copper bottoms consumed the most time and money. If a ship's bottom was fouled with barnacles and other marine organisms, the whaler might be "heaved down," or hauled over on her side with a great tackle so that the crew could scrape and scrub it clean. Open seams were filled with fresh oakum, and the copper plates, which offered protection from the destructive toredo mollusk, were replaced and renailed as required. It cost approximately $2,000 to caulk and copper a whaleship.

In the printed company instructions, the owners explicitly warned the ship captains to keep spending in line. Masters were to enter all financial transactions in an account book, and they usually filed a copy of every receipt and expense chit in the ship's document box, to substantiate outlays on returning home. During the course of a voyage, in keeping with the owners' desires, the captains generally sent a letter from each port they visited, giving a rough idea of the nature and amount of expenses incurred. If he could not sell enough of his oil or bone to cover the cost of repairing and recruiting, the captain had the authority to execute drafts on the owners' treasurers, Willets & Co., for the amounts he required.

Being thrifty Yankee businessmen, the Cold Spring shipowners took a very dim view of extravagance, which required the captains constantly to alibi and excuse in their letter reports. Captain William James Grant was roundly criticized in a letter from John H. Jones during the 1854 voyage of the *Huntsville*. Grant, in return, apologized for not having sent duplicates of his disbursements, but noted that, "You will find that I am very particular in My transaction of business and in the selection of advisers, before any transactions take place. . . . I make my own selections before purchasing and know that I am buying at the lowest possible price—it is my daily occupation from morning until night."

Expenses plagued Captain Grant for the entire voyage. It began at Honolulu in November 1855, when he sent home $4,400 in bills, covering such items and services as caulking ship and procuring bread, hemp rigging for the jib stay, flying jib guys, a new spar and a number of other expenses which had not been anticipated. Grant wrote that, ". . . You May be astonished at My Bills at first sight, but in the End You will be satisfied because they are honest things obtained in this place. . . ." He was careful to mention that it was impossible to sell anything on board for the "ship trade" and he decided to hold his oil on board since it was commanding only 45 cents per gallon there in Honolulu, against an average of $1.77 per gallon back home.

It was difficult to decide which grounds to exploit for a new season because Honolulu was rife with varying rumors of, perhaps, good whaling off New Zealand, the Japan Sea, or possibly for the moment Kodiak or Kamchatka were enjoying popularity. A cautious captain made the rounds, canvassing ship chandlers, merchants, and ships' agents for information on especially greasy, or lucky, grounds. Then, they usually consulted with other masters who happened to be in port, or eavesdropped on the scuttlebutt and rumors in the dockside taverns. The ultimate decision of the cruising ground fell squarely on the captain's shoulders, and he was sure to be damned and scorned by the owners, officers and crew alike if he brought the ship back empty at the end of a season.

During the winter the South Seas islands were delightful places in which to recruit. Whenever they put into one of those palm studded atolls, the whalers were always greeted by natives who came out in scores of outrigger canoes which were loaded with coconuts, bananas, oranges, lemons and breadfruit, as well as yams and other vegetables and live pigs and chickens. The sailors offered trinkets and trade goods for what they wanted and the bartering was often spirited.

A number of these South Seas islands, during the whaling days, were inhabited by cannibals, or at the very least by natives who were none too friendly to roving whalers. In the fall of 1851 the *Sheffield* put in to San Cristobal, one of the Solomons, and was approached by almost a hundred two-man canoes. The captain bought some fruit from the islanders in trade for little pieces of iron hoop, but when he got underway again they ". . . yelled like demons, and fired their arrows at our sails, seemingly in the utmost anger at our leaving. . . ." Strangely enough, one man—sitting alone in his canoe—hung onto a a line trailing from the ship's stern, happily singing and apparently enjoying the ride, even though he was being taken out to sea. Then, about ten miles out, he cast off and calmly paddled back to the island.

A short time later the *Sheffield* touched at Ascension Island, where Captain Roys discovered his brother Sam, who was mate aboard the New Bedford whaling brig *Inga*. The brother told him that the captain, Thomas D. Barnes, was in the habit of trading with the natives and allowed them to come on board in great numbers without taking any precautions.

Roys did not agree with Captain Barnes' lax ways, and induced Sam to join him aboard the *Sheffield*. And it is well he did, for as fate would have it, when the brig touched at Pleasant Island a short time later, the natives boarded the ship and killed everyone except a crewman named James Blair and a Kanaka, who managed to jump overboard and escape. The natives plundered the ship and set it afire, but Blair and the Kanaka were able to slip back aboard and steal out of sight of the island, bound on a course for Sydney, Australia. Two men were no match for a 160-ton ship and she was soon dismasted. The two drifted aimlessly for six weeks more, until picked up by a passing ship and landed at Honolulu.

Cold Spring ships called at over forty ports and islands on five continents, but the most unusual, for that particular time, was an unexpected visit to Japan by the *Splendid* during her 1848 cruise to the Pacific. Captain Mercator Cooper, in 1845, had been one of the first whalers allowed to visit the Empire of Japan. Sailing in the Sag Harbor ship *Manhattan,* he visited that country at a time when it was closed to trade with foreigners. *Splendid* is believed to have been the second American whaler legally to enter Japan, and the circumstances were very unusual. While cruising off the islands north of Japan she discovered a junk which had been abandoned in a typhoon. Captain Pierson took the strange craft in tow and put into the nearest Japanese port, where some officials came on board and had every man removed from the ship. They were then marched to a picturesque park, bathed in a pool and dressed in Oriental costumes. From there they were led to a banquet hall where a great feast awaited them, with each course served by separate groups of women in different kimonos. After the meal, the sailors were taken back to the pool, bathed again, dressed in their own clothing and marched back to the ship, where they were told "to go to sea" and if they "ever entered a Japanese port again, every man would be beheaded." The junk had a cargo of tea, so each man took a chest of it for himself. A few years later, in 1854, Commodore Matthew Calbraith Perry negotiated the famous treaty which opened Japan to American trade.

7

Tales of Bravery and Gallant Rescue

THE SEA has continually taken a toll of men and ships, and the Cold Spring whalers distinguished themselves by bravery and humanity toward shipwrecked fellow mariners. Captain William S. Beebe of the *Alice* helped rescue the crew of the New Bedford whaler *Polar Star* when she was wrecked on the eastern shore of the Okhotsk Sea on May 22, 1861. *Alice* was sailing northerly between the ice and land off the west coast of Kamchatka in company with five other whaleships. At nightfall, Beebe hove to under shortened sail, believing the ship to be about 23 miles from land. Suddenly someone noticed that the *Polar Star,* and another whaleship, the *Oliver Crocker,* were wearing rather close to shore. It was later learned that Captain David Cochran of the *Oliver Crocker* thought there was fifty miles of sea room between the pack ice and shore, but taking no chances, decided to stay close to the ice. At 11:00 P.M. Cochran suddenly felt her shudder. He dashed up the ladderway, but before he could reach the deck the vessel struck twice again. The captain immediately asked if they were in the ice pack, but the mate excitedly answered that there was no ice in sight, so the ship must have struck bottom.

Captain Cochran then looked astern and gasped when he saw the *Polar Star* half a mile off, running directly for the shore. Daniel D. Wood, her captain, probably thought he was skirting the pack ice, for the shore there is very deceiving. Cochran later admitted that he too had thought that the low lying land, covered with snow, was floating ice. Despite some urgent maneuvers, *Polar Star* was blown hard ashore. Her crew tried diligently to get off, cutting away the spars to ease her, but the heavy seas drove her even closer to shore, where the helpless vessel soon bilged and filled with water. At 3:00 A.M. the *Oliver Crocker* came bearing down on *Alice,* her ensign at half-mast and lamps aglow, and when alongside, the *Crocker*'s people shouted over the news that the *Polar Star* was aground.

Soon, both ships were in company under full sail, beating toward the wreck, hampered somewhat by a strong northerly current, a heavy sea and the threatening ice pack. Their progress was agonizingly slow until the weather finally moderated. At approximately 4:00 P.M., the *Alice* and *Oliver Crocker* were able to get near enough to rescue Captain Wood and his crew, who had taken to the ship's boats. The officers and men were then divided between the two rescue ships, which stood offshore for the night. The following morning they came abreast of the wreck and anchored in eleven fathoms of water. Parties from both ships went ashore, and the wreck was sold at auction for $200 to Captain Cochran of the *Oliver Crocker,* who was the highest bidder. The officers and crewmen were able to save most of their personal gear, but very little could be salvaged from the wreck itself, because the salvagers could work only at half tides, with the rescue ships lying about 10 miles away. When the pack ice began to get dangerously thick, the captains wisely decided to give up any further salvage attempts.

As whaling captains went, Isaac Ludlow was a man of interesting contrasts. He was hard as nails to some of his crews, yet he had heart enough to give up an entire whaling season in order to take 105 stranded souls, shipwrecked on a desolate rock in the Indian Ocean, back to civilization. In 1845, his stern policies obviously a contributing factor, Captain Ludlow killed a man while quashing a mutiny aboard the Sag Harbor whaler *Oscar,* while at Ilha Grande, Brazil. For this he was charged with homicide, but amidst loud public outcry was never indicted. After this bitter and trying experience, Captain Ludlow remained ashore for a year to regain his perspective, and finally took command of the *Arabella* out of Sag Harbor in 1847. This voyage brightened his spirits somewhat, for he returned in July 1849 with a cargo of 50 barrels of sperm oil, 2,000 barrels of whale oil and 10,500 pounds of whalebone. Again, he went ashore with his family for two years before taking *Monmouth* out of Cold Spring on August 28, 1851. He worked the Atlantic grounds that fall, touching at Fayal in early October and Tristan da Cuhna in December. During 1852 *Monmouth* cruised into the Indian Ocean and worked those grounds on-and-off for about a year.

While *Monmouth* was searching the Indian Ocean for whales, the 529-ton British packet *Meridian* was fitting out at Gravesend, England, for an emigrant voyage to Australia. She sailed on June 4, 1853, with 84 passengers (26 men, 17 women and 41 children under 16 years) and a cargo worth about £25,000, bound for Sydney. *Meridian* was a first class vessel, just a year old, built with stout timbers and fittings of oak and teak and excellent ironwork. She was as strong as wood and metal could make her. *Meridian* was skippered by Captain Richard T. Hernaman, an able and experienced navigator, who had taken her to Australia on her maiden voyage in 1852. Always alert, courteous and attentive to passengers and crew, Hernaman was proud that in 15 years as a master he had never lost even a single spar overboard.

Meridian did not carry as many passengers as she might have accommodated on this particular voyage because freight to Sydney was commanding a very good price. The managing owner was so intent to fill the ship with cargo rather than people that he did not consider the comfort or safety of the passengers at all. If it was not for Captain Hernaman's tact and good humor, there would have been a good deal of discontent. As it was, some of the passengers vowed to publish an advertisement in the Sydney newspapers, strongly protesting the manner in which the ship had been fitted out, provisioned and manned. They were especially displeased with the 23-man crew, because, exclusive of the captain and the 3 mates, there were only 10 experienced seamen among the lot. This shortage of qualified hands made it impossible to maintain a regular watch forward, for, with a man at the wheel and another in the fo'c's'le, the lookout would have to leave his post and come aft to assist whenever they decided to make a maneuver. There was no boatswain and the mates had to man the ropes just like common sailors in addition to their duties as ship's officers. In clear weather even the passengers helped tend lines and halliards, but because of their lack of experience were precluded from assisting at night and in bad weather, when their help was most needed.

It was fine going until *Meridian* reached latitude 20° S, where she ran in with baffling winds, calms and squalls, and then a brief, stiff gale. On the night of August 23, while running for St. Paul's Island, which the captain wanted to sight in order to correct a suspected chronometer error, they encountered a strong gale, and altered course for the island of Amsterdam which lies about sixty miles due north of St. Paul's. The gale continued throughout the night. During the following day they passed the bark *John Sugars,* which Captain Hernaman immediately determined had left London for Sydney two weeks before *Meridian.* Spurred, no doubt, by a good bit of professional pride, despite an already near record passage, Hernaman ignored the thick weather and bad chronometer and ordered a course change, so that his vessel could sail faster before the wind.

Hernaman told the passengers that he expected to raise Amsterdam about midnight, and directed Mr. Lamburd, the first mate, who had the watch, to keep a sharp lookout. He should have realized, however, that the mate and the rest of the officers and crew were very tired after having been up the entire night before. And instead of posting a fo'c's'le watch, at approximately 7:00 P.M. the captain changed to a smoother course and foolishly ordered the entire watch to bail water out of his partially flooded cabin. Minutes later, a smart shock threw everyone to the decks and sent the ship quivering from stem to stern. At first they thought that there had been a collision, but after five or six more violent shocks, the sickening, grating sound of rocks against the bottom quickly told the bitter truth.

Soon the children were screaming and everyone was running about in utter confusion, terror and despair. When *Meridian* had first struck, Captain Hernaman came rushing up the poop ladderway, shouting three times, "Where is Mr. Lamburd?" Reaching the quarterdeck, he quickly realized she was aground, and looking up, exclaimed, "My God! It is the island!" Seizing the wheel, the captain tried to put the helm hard to starboard, but the vessel again struck violently. "Now every man for himself," he shouted. A few seconds later a heavy sea burst over the poop and swept the captain, and a seaman named Charles Snow, overboard. Snow fortunately was able to grab a line and pulled himself to safety. Captain Hernaman was never seen again.

Meanwhile, Mr. Lamburd and some crewmen climbed into the masttops, while others grasped the rigging and braced themselves against the full fury of the wild seas. The carpenter, axe in hand, asked Lamburd what to do, but was told, "I do not know; do what you like." It was clear that the wavering masts had to be cut to relieve the ship, but the carpenter did not want to override a superior officer, so the ship was left to the mercy of the rocks and breakers.

'Tween decks there was absolute pandemonium among the passengers. Now the ship listed severely to port, and with every sea which swept the decks, more water began to flood the second cabin. Somehow they all managed to work their way through neckdeep water to the starboard side, which was still above water. Pity the poor children, some of whom had already been put to bed, who asked rather innocently whether the voyage was over, or if "Aunt Sarah would have a good fire, as it was very wet." Huddled together, fearing the worst, the second cabin families remained 'tween decks until about 9:30 P.M. when the second mate, third mate and a seaman, at the risk of their lives, went below to rescue them. The task took about an hour to complete, with the three men constantly dodging cargo which was floating in the 'tween deck. They finished just as it looked as if the vessel was going to break up. The lower deck had already collapsed. The last person to be taken out, a woman, slipped and fell into the hold. Horribly bruised, she was pulled out by two of her children. Charles Snow bravely descended into the hold and brought the mother and children the rest of the way up the companion ladder, which was washed away just as the woman placed her foot on deck.

The chief cabin passengers, the younger children still in their nightshirts, all drenched to the skins and shivering with cold, huddled in the galley and the steward's pantry. Gradually their initial fears faded, and they became resigned to their plight. Although safe for the moment, the passengers got nothing but ominous silence from the officers and crew, and worse yet could not see anything through the murky night, hearing only the terrible groaning of the ship's timbers against the jagged rocks. Someone then suggested that it might be best to remain aboard until the ship began to break up, and then they could ride the pieces ashore as best they could.

About 11:00 P.M. the mizzen mast began to spring loose, and the people feared that its fall would hurl them all to destruction. Gradually, the ship began to break in two, which lessened the strain on the after part. About 1:30 A.M. the mainmast split, but by amazing good fortune, it fell toward the boulders on shore, forming a perfect bridge across the menacing breakers which had previously prevented anyone from reaching the island. The sailors, true to previous mettle, ran across first but were quickly followed by some younger passengers and a few married couples. The cowardly seamen would not assist the passengers ashore, but Mr. Worthington, the third mate, promised that he would not leave until everyone was safely ashore, telling them, "Remain where you are . . . be of good cheer—you will be saved—the vessel will hold together." In the morning, he and Charles Snow passed repeatedly from ship to shore—buffeted several times by heavy seas—helping anyone willing to go ashore.

Meanwhile, Mr. Tulloch, the second mate, was comforting and assisting the people who had already crossed. It took considerable time to coax the women to cross, but by 3:00 A.M., with the water in the saloon rising quickly, everyone realized that it was time to abandon ship. As if by a miracle all 105 souls were rescued by dawn. There were three men lost; the captain, the ship's feeble old cook, Thomas George, and a Swiss steerage passenger named Pfau. All three were washed overboard soon after *Meridian* struck.

When dawn broke, the survivors were appalled at the sight before them. Huge boulders were piled irregularly from forty to fifty feet high and backed by a three to four hundred foot wall of black rock, which looked impossible to scale. Turning seaward, they saw little left of the once-proud *Meridian* save for a small portion of the fo'c's'le and the after portion of the hull with the mizzen canted towards shore. The rest of the ship was completely broken to pieces which were being thrust on the rocks by the tremendous breakers. Meanwhile, the sailors set a fire to warm themselves and the passengers and distributed some dry clothing which had been salvaged from the cargo. They were a curious sight—men, women and children—dressed in ill-fitting red and blue woolen shirts and baggy ready-made trousers which were originally consigned to the gold diggers in Australia.

The island of Amsterdam is actually an extinct volcano, some 24 miles in circumference, rising almost 3,000 feet from the sea. It was out of the track of ships bound for Australia, which usually shaped their courses at least two to three degrees more to the southward, to take advantage of westerly winds which generally prevail in higher latitudes. In the past, Amsterdam had been a haunt of whalers, but the animals were becoming scarce, so much so, that by 1852 only two ships worked that ground. The island was uninhabited and barren, except for some wild cabbage, originally planted by the shipwrecked crew of a French vessel. If the surf was not running too high, a few mollusks could be gathered along the rocks by the shore, and there were plenty of sea birds, as well as abundant fish. Here they were stranded with little powder and shot to hunt birds, nothing with which to catch fish and no tools to build a boat, which probably could not have been launched anyway. The weather, which was almost always poor, consisted of five or six days of rain and storm for each day of sunshine.

Not surprisingly, Mr. Lamburd was no help at all, and on the first day ashore he seemed completely overwhelmed by the situation. The chief mate had taken no part in the rescue of the women and children from the ship, claiming illness. He neither gave orders to the seamen nor example to the passengers, so everyone did as he pleased. With a little direction some of the crew and passengers might have tried to save some provisions from the wreck. But the foolish seamen, and even a few passengers, began to plunder the ship, while others, more sensibly, tried—somewhat aimlessly—to save the provisions. When some of them found part of the ship's wine and spirits, they attempted to drown their predicament in drink.

A lawyer named Alfred Lutwyche tried to find a way up the steep cliff above them, but was unsuccessful. During his absence he had been elected storekeeper for the group. He reluctantly accepted the thankless and damnable duty of having to divide the meager provisions among the 105 hungry people. A natural leader, he soon had the passengers and seamen gathering up everything edible, which was brought to protected spots under some boulders. But by evening they had gathered only two soggy bags of biscuits, several tins of salted red herring, two or three pieces of salt beef and a few bottles of port wine. Each adult therefore was allowed one biscuit and every child half a biscuit for that day, with herring being distributed to the few who would eat them without fresh water. Each woman and child got a half a glass of wine, with none for the men, some of whom had already had more than their fill anyway. That night a makeshift tent of a torn sail and some boards from the wreck was pitched for a few women and children, while the rest huddled together on the mist covered rocks.

The following morning (Friday, August 26) the men, hoping to get their blood circulating again, were much more willing to work than the day previous. A party went west about a mile and a half from the wreck and found fresh water, while another, going eastward, tried to find a way to ascend the cliff. The seamen, meanwhile, seeming a little ashamed of their previous conduct, decided to help look for provisions. In the afternoon, the party which had gone eastward somehow got to the top of the cliff. Once there, they dropped guide ropes below, enabling others to climb to the crest. By evening, a number of crewmen, the dead captain's wife and daughter and a few passengers were up and had pitched camp by a clear stream. The remainder stayed below for the night, kept awake by a great fire which was blazing somewhere above them. The next day they learned that a drunken seaman had set some reeds afire "to clear the ground a little," forcing the people on the cliff to run about the entire night, whenever the wind shifted, to avoid being scorched by the flames.

By now many of the women and children were shoeless and cramped and chilled by the cold, exposure and lack of exercise, so the men decided to get the rest of them up the cliff by the following day. The men pulled themselves up the precipice by two ropes, while the women and children were hauled up the 300 feet of perpendicular rock by a rope tied around their waists. By the end of the 27th, only Lamburd and Lutwyche remained below to tend the stores.

Despite strict rationing, there were only enough biscuits for a week, along with a few cases of preserved meats, a canister half full of preserved potatoes, a large canister of tea, 5 or 6 pieces of salt beef, 2 hams, about 25 cases of herring, 2 small casks of brandy and a few bottles of port, claret and champagne, a box of raisins, about 2 dozen candles, 5 boxes of matches, 2 double barreled guns, a six-shot revolver, 2 pistols and 5 flasks of gunpowder. This was all they had to support 105 people, which included a lot of women and children who could not help themselves. Fortunately, about 6 or 7 dozen whale-birds—half-roasted by the fire the previous evening—were gathered up and someone found one of the ship's pigs, which had drowned and washed within reach of shore. On Monday and Tuesday Lutwyche was able to issue a ration consisting of a half-pound of pork, a small handful of raisins, half a moldy biscuit, a little tea and some brandy. Unknown to the others, the first mate and a few of the crewmen and passengers had secreted their own private caches of food.

On Sunday Lutwyche told the first mate he thought they should move the stores to the top of the cliff, and then engage all hands to look under large pieces of the wreck for more provisions, which were obviously there. Lamburd disagreed, arguing that it was his "duty" to protect Lutwyche and the stores, and some booty they had gathered, with his double-barreled gun. The lawyer could not believe that any of the ship's company would harm them, but he could see the first mate's point, for most of the seamen were either roaming about the shore looking for loot, or ransacking the wreck. Wisely, Lutwyche thought that this was no time to argue the question of ownership. While some of the passengers were setting up tents and huts or fashioning clothing, others amused themselves by hunting or attempting to ascend the volcanic mountain. Their efforts were aborted by a jungle of thick cane some five to eight feet high. One of the hunters, upon returning to camp, reported seeing a ship far off on the horizon. There was still some hope of rescue!

On the morning of the 29th the whole camp was excited. A ship was rounding the point, having twice answered signals on the cliff by lowering her ensign. It was simply amazing that she should be at an island which was seldom sighted, much less visited. Everyone was overjoyed and signaling from every quarter, and with the aid of a spyglass saved from the wreck, they soon determined that she was beating right for the island. Despair became tumult and excitement, as the grass, what was left of it, was again set fire to guide the approaching vessel. Everyone was waving something—even the shirts from their backs—in hopes that the ship would positively see them. Gradually, she bore closer and closer, finally answering their now frantic signals by sending up her colors. She was a whaler of about 300 tons! After a while the ship tacked and tried to stand in, but the wind was blowing so far from the land that she was compelled to go out to sea. The ship made another tack, but again was obliged to stand out to sea. Everyone was disappointed to see the little vessel sail out of sight, but continued to hope that she would return to take them off, or at the very least, leave some provisions.

Unfortunately, the crew and able-bodied passengers, anticipating immediate relief, did not continue to search for more provisions or even bring those already collected to the top of the cliff. That night the weather worsened, and comber after comber pounded the crevices where the stores were kept. Lutwyche and Lamburd, dragging a little of the more perishable food with them, reached higher ground just as the rollers became one continuous line as far as they could see, smashing and dispersing the remains of the wreck, thereby dashing any hope of finding further provisions. The gale increased and the breakers reached higher and higher, threatening the two men, who now had every reason to believe that they would soon be dashed away. Finally, on the morning of the 30th, the storm subsided and they were pleased to find that the stores below were practically **undamaged.** Most of the pile of timbers, and the provisions which were probably under it, were gone, while the mizzen mast had given way and all that remained of the *Meridian* was the outer planking from the poop, which had been driven nearly on end toward the rocks.

Atop the cliff almost all of the tents were blown down. The first mate was obviously incompetent, so it was time for someone to take overall charge. Although he had no right to, Mr. Lutwyche gave the first order and had Lamburd summon the men to bring the provisions to the top of the cliff. Within two hours everything was safe, with the exception of the brandy, some silver coin and other treasure, which Lamburd continued to guard, while Lutwyche distributed rations. Exhausted, but accepted as the leader by the ship's company, Lutwyche finally was able to lie down under cover to sleep for the first time since the wreck.

The sailors stayed to themselves at one end of the encampment, in order to hide provisions and goods they had taken secretly, while the passengers settled in tents and huts on the opposite side of the stream which ran through the area. They found an abundance of peat for fuel, but had few cooking utensils, save for a large tin footbath, which served as a cauldron for the whole camp, some empty sardine and herring tins, a few cups and saucers and several knives.

By the following day, Wednesday, August 31, the whaler still had not reappeared, but failing to give up hope, a party was sent out to find a good place for a boat to land. With rations for two days, three of the best seamen and the carpenter set out on this vital mission. While the men were getting ready, the morning's rations for the ship's company, consisting of a handful of moldy biscuit crumbs, a baked apple, some tea and a glass of wine, were issued. They had just finished eating, about 10:00 A.M., when someone shouted, "A boat! A boat!" Sure enough, it was a whaleboat near shore, rowing a safe distance from the surf. The boatheader had a waif or flag in his hand, which he waved and gestured two or three times towards the direction from which they had come. The people on the cliff signaled that they undersood, so the boat headed back to the ship.

There was hope, joy and lots of activity on the cliff. Help was not long in coming! But it would not arrive just yet, for a heavy wind sprang up, causing the boat's crew some difficulty in returning to the ship. The ship stood out to sea immediately, and when the gale died down—two days later—the whalemen were about eighty miles from the island. Meanwhile, the majority of the *Meridian*'s crew had left in pursuit of the exploring party. Mr. Lutwyche, perhaps somewhat unjustly, did not fully trust them, suspecting they might not tell the whaler's captain that there were a number of people stranded on the island. As a precaution, he sent a French passenger named Henry Dehan on their heels, and later set out himself with a list of the survivors, so that the whaling captain would have some idea of the assistance and accomodations which would be required.

It would be difficult for the passengers, few of whom had decent boots or shoes, or any foot protection for that matter, to walk a dangerous and uneven path to the debarkation point. They could not penetrate the thick brush, so had to inch dangerously close to the edge of the cliff. It took most of the train of half-famished, footsore women and children three days to cover a distance of only twelve miles. A few took four days to make the journey, while two stragglers completed it in five days. Fathers and mothers with infants tied to their backs were forced to rest frequently, nourishing themselves only with a herring a day and a spot of water. Their scant clothes afforded little protection against violent hail storms, and bone-chilling winds. It was a miserable, tortuous trip.

On the evening of the second day, everybody had just settled down for the night, when suddenly a tall, powerful man, dressed in sailor's garb, appeared on the brow of a nearby hill. He announced that he was William Smith, mate of the boat they had seen the day before. He had been landed by Captain Isaac Ludlow of the Cold Spring bark *Monmouth,* who had seen their distress signals through his spyglass. This was a stroke of incredibly good luck, for it is said that the *Monmouth* was the only whaleship operating in the area, and she had been a fortnight early in arriving. Smith told the party that there was a place to board the boats only a mile away, and if they were willing to walk that little distance there would be plenty of good bread and meat for all. Everyone jumped to their feet and previous exhaustion soon vanished. Although he had misjudged the distance, purposely perhaps, Smith did everything possible to make the passengers comfortable, assurring them that Captain Ludlow would try to take every man, woman and child from the island. On arriving at the spot Smith mentioned, they were very disappointed that the salt pork and biscuit he had promised were not there. It was later learned that Captain Ludlow was unable to land the food because of the gale and was driven out to sea again. Now there would be nothing to eat but some wild cabbages from a nearby patch.

Saturday and Sunday, the 3rd and 4th of September, passed with still no sign of the ship. Food was desperately short, and the raw cabbage was beginning to make some of the women and children sick. The men wanted to gather some limpets from the rocks, but were forced back by the high waves. By Sunday night their plight was critical. A water hole nearby had failed, and the nearest fresh water was at least a mile away, with only boots or wine bottles to carry it back. Even the cabbage was running out. Then, at daybreak on Monday, Smith woke the entire encampment with a tremendous shout. "Ship! Ship!," he exclaimed in a booming voice. There was the *Monmouth* standing in by shore!

Captain Ludlow, a tall, commanding man, was soon on shore, shaking hands with the excited people clustered around him. He had just landed in his own boat, followed by his second mate, William Brower, who brought some biscuits and a piece of pork, which were quickly distributed among the famished survivors. Ludlow, fearing that not a moment's time could be lost, would not allow anyone to sit down to eat. He led the way to the boats which lay a quarter of a mile off, with the entire ragged ship's company straggling behind him. Arriving there, they found the waters remarkably calm. The rocks at this point jut out, forming sort of a natural wharf, and Captain Ludlow was the only person aboard the *Monmouth* who had known of its existence.

Four whaleboats were needed to take the survivors away. The women and children went first, and by noon all were safely aboard, except for a little girl that the Chief Steward was carrying on his back. They were taken off the following day, but one person, a steerage passenger named Pell was still back at the original camp. This man, drunk the first day after the wreck, had severely injured his foot on the rocks and could not travel. He had been left with a good stock of provisions at the crest of the cliff. Capain Ludlow sent four whalers, including Smith, to fetch him, declaring he could not think of leaving even one man on the island, so long as a pound of bread remained on the ship. This could have been a difficult decision, for foul weather could have delayed completion of the rescue for days or even weeks. Sure enough, another gale came up on Tuesday, September 6, forcing the ship to put out to sea again, until Friday, when, with some difficulty, the captain himself manned the boat which took Pell and the four whalers off. It turned out that they had to carry the injured man the entire distance on their backs, and had reached the debarkation point only on Thursday night. With three cheers for the determined captain and his brave crew, they made all sail for Mauritius.

The survivors were treated generously and sympathetically throughout the voyage by the captain, his mates and the rest of the ship's hard-pressed crew, even though each had forfeited his share in a whaling season. It must have been especially disappointing, because the *Monmouth* had been out for two years and had not been very successful, being only half full of oil at the time she arrived off the island of Amsterdam. She might well have filled her holds there, for a number of whales were seen offshore, with one breaking water not an eighth of a mile from a boat which took survivors to the ship. Yet not a murmur was heard from any of the whalemen, despite the sacrifice of their livelihood and literally taking bread out of their mouths to feed the *Meridian*'s people, who said that the food was better than that which was served aboard British packets. They had their fill of the best of biscuits, salt beef, pork, fresh rice from Java, pure spring water, yams, sweet potatoes and molasses, supplemented by fresh fish and a couple of porpoises, which even the ladies had to admit, once they had overcome their prejudices, were excellent, palatable food.

The children received lots of attention and regained weight rapidly, and before the voyage was half over they were as noisy and troublesome as ever. There was little privacy for anyone. Many of the women were unable to change clothes until the ship reached port, but two were fortunate enough to share Captain Ludlow's cabin, while he slept on the deck. The majority of the passengers either slept in the hold, using some old sails for bedding, or on the decks. A few had the use of berths and hammocks, which the sailors had generously given up. Everyone was ready to admit that this was far better than the hard rocks and wet reeds back on Amsterdam.

Monmouth finally came to anchor off Port Louis, Mauritius, on Monday, September 26, after a fine, but rather long passage of seventeen days. The passengers were prepared to beg the government and people of Mauritius for sympathy and assistance, and the next morning the captain's boat took several of them ashore. They were directed to the office of the Colonial Secretary where they were received with kindness and attention by everyone. The government steamer transported the passengers to the quarantine, where bread, butter, tea, cheese and sugar were waiting. Meanwhile, the private sector was busy at work. The men of the Colonial Secretary's office collected clothing from their personal friends, and before the evening closed a large bundle was brought down to the station.

Some townspeople took in whole families, providing them with everything they needed at no expense. Men and women scurried about, collecting about £400 worth of clothing, sending whole bales down to the quarantine station. A fund was initiated for the survivors by the Chamber of Commerce. In all, over £1,300 was collected—an enormous sum for a place so small.

On October 3 the passengers called a public meeting, at which they passed a series of resolutions expressing their gratitude to Captain Ludlow, his officers and crew, as well as to Edward Tulloch and Leonard Worthington, the second and third mates, and seaman Charles Snow of the *Meridian*. The Governor and inhabitants of Mauritius were gratefully thanked for their generosity. Then, as a testimonial to Captain Ludlow, somehow they scraped together £27 to purchase a suitably inscribed watch.

The Colonial Secretary sent a flattering letter to Captain Ludlow, stating that the Governor hoped to be authorized by her Majesty's Government to indemnify him for the lost whaling season and also to present him with a testimonial "which may endure to record exertions, of which it could not pretend to be a recompense." Ludlow, in responding, asked that the Governor be given "my warmest thanks for the very kind sentiments he has expressed," adding that "I shall always enjoy through the rest of my life, the pleasing recollections and satisfaction that I have done my duty to God and Man, and a duty we all owe to one another, when placed in such circumstances. . . ."

It is said that the Governor gave a ball in honor of Captain Ludlow and his crew. The Chamber of Commerce subscribed £130 for a service of plate for him, but he preferred to use the money as a trust fund for his nine children. Mr. Tulloch and Mr. Worthington, the mates of the *Meridian,* were each presented with gold medals and £25, but for some unexplained reason seaman Snow was not recognized. The local newspaper suspiciously noticed that there was no praise for the rest of the *Meridian*'s crew, and inferred that they had left "infant children and their mothers to shift for themselves when they were so near the brink of death. . . ."

Captain Ludlow's unusual humility pervaded the entire affair, and he continually brushed aside much of the praise, saying, "I have done no more than my duty." His letter, written just before leaving Mauritius, to the owners in Cold Spring is a masterpiece of succinctness:

Isle of France, Oct. 18th, 1853

Mr. Walter R. Jones—My dear Sir:

What will you think, when I tell you that I have lost a season of Whaling around the Island of Amsterdam, by having to take the crew and passengers of the Meridian, of London, bound for Sydney, which ship was wrecked on the night of the 24th of August last, on the southwest part of the Island, amounting in all to 105 [persons].

These people I have brought here after a passage of 17 days. I think you will exonerate me from all blame when you hear the story of the sad loss of the ill fated ship and the salvation of the suffering passengers and crew. I suppose you will have a full account of the whole soon after you get this letter, should it reach you. Dear Sir, I know well that I have lost a season of Whaling around the land where we should most likely have taken 500 or 600 barrels of oil, but when you know that through one of your ships . . . 105 British subjects have been saved from sure destruction, I think you will feel it a high privilege instead of a loss. . . .

Isaac Ludlow

That same day Captain Ludlow submitted a claim to the Government of Mauritius for almost $1,200 for replenishing water and provisions which were consumed by the survivors of the *Meridian*. The Governor readily agreed to pay the claim, and after a little red tape, had the amount credited to the *Monmouth*. Captain Ludlow sailed on October 24, with every ship in the harbor decorated for the occasion, while ashore guns were fired, bells rung and people cheered.

News of Captain Ludlow's bravery spread quickly throughout the civilized world. The London *Morning Chronicle* praised the "rare sacrifice on the part of the crew of the *Monmouth*." And the *Illustrated London News* published a detailed pictorial account by one of the *Meridian*'s passengers. The news of the rescue reached New York by mid-December.

In January 1854 a fine gold watch, with an engraved sentiment, was received at home by Captain Ludlow's wife, Phoebe. Coming from London, it was the timepiece the passengers had promised to send during their meeting at Mauritius. Accompanying the watch was $620 which had been collected by the people of Port Louis for the purchase of a piece of silver plate as a "testimonial of [Captain Ludlow's] humane and heroic conduct. . . ." Mrs. Ludlow wrote a letter of thanks the very same day, promising that although, "My husband is still absent . . . I shall lose no time in making him acquainted with the safe arrival at his own home of these touching evidences of gratitude. . . ."

SILVER MEDAL
Presented to each member of the crew of the *Monmouth* for their part in the rescue of 105 survivors of the *Meridian*, wrecked in 1853 on the Island of Amsterdam.

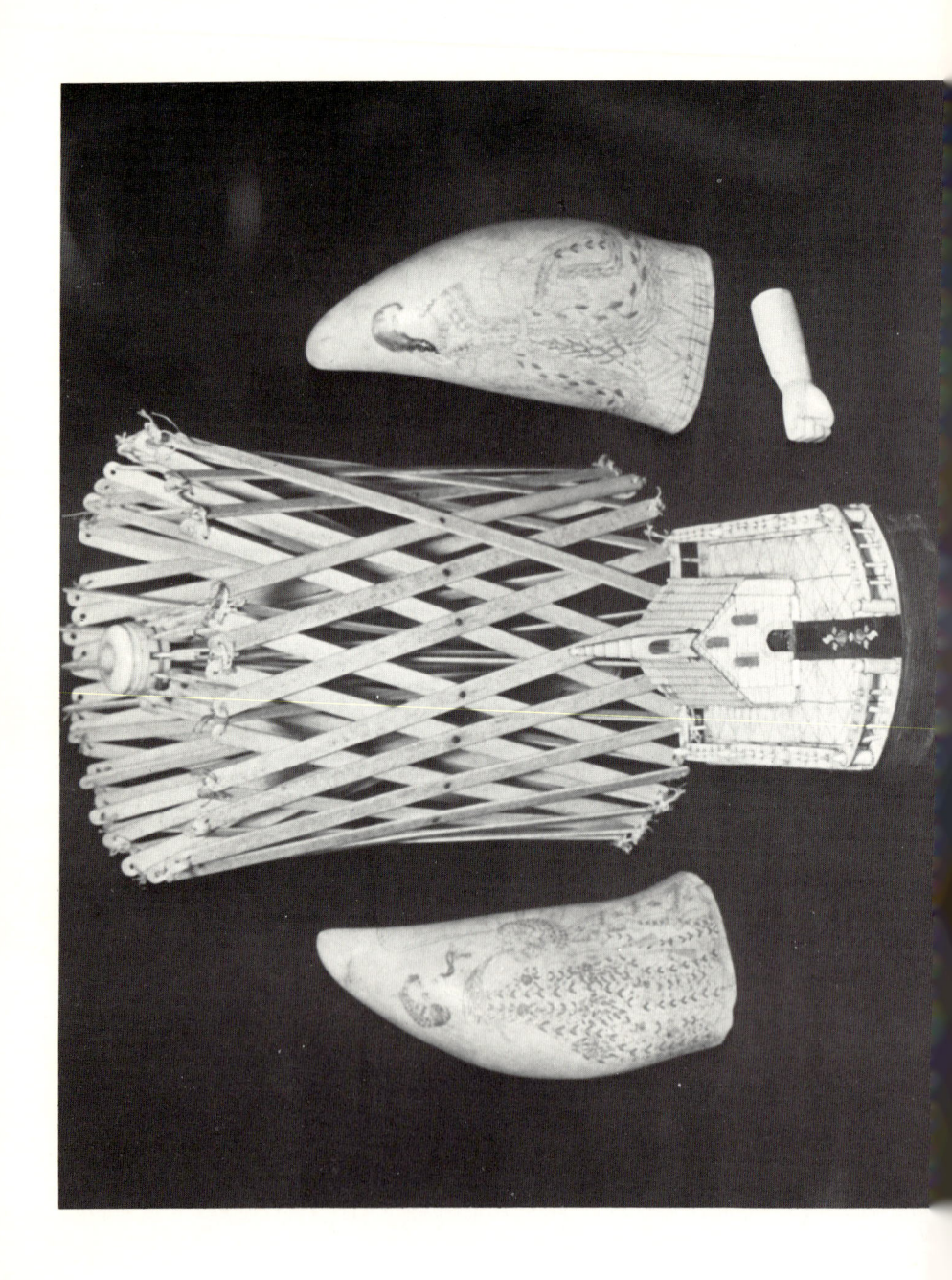

SCRIMSHAW
These local examples include a pair of sperm whale teeth engraved by Captain Enos, a whalebone swift for winding yarn, a model of St. John's Church at Cold Spring Harbor, and a small ivory hand.

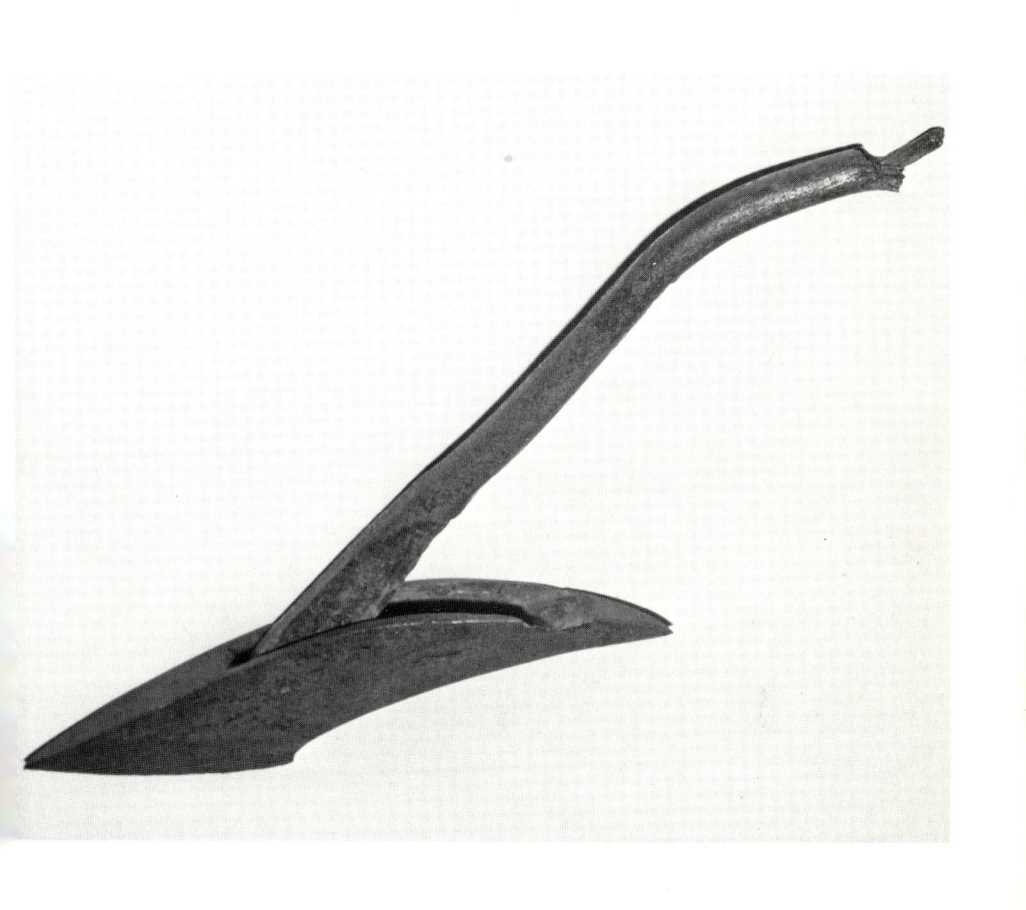

A TOGGLE IRON
Marked with the name of the *Alice* was found years after it had become embedded in a whale and snapped off. The animal was caught by the San Francisco whaler *Andrew Hicks*.

The next four illustrations are taken from woodcuts which appeared with Peter Dumont's narrative of a voyage in the *Monmouth*. The story appeared in Frank Leslie's *Illustrated Newspaper*, March 26, 1859.

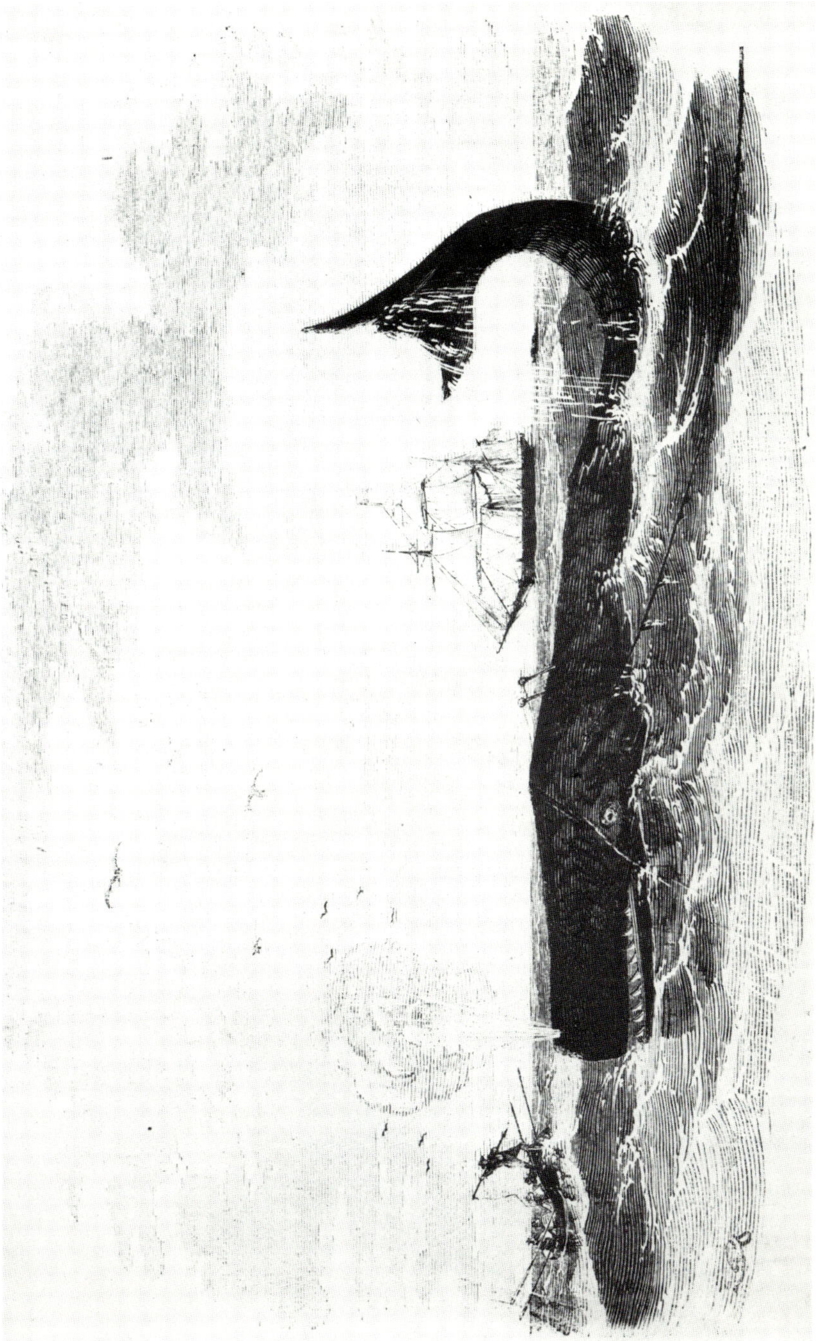

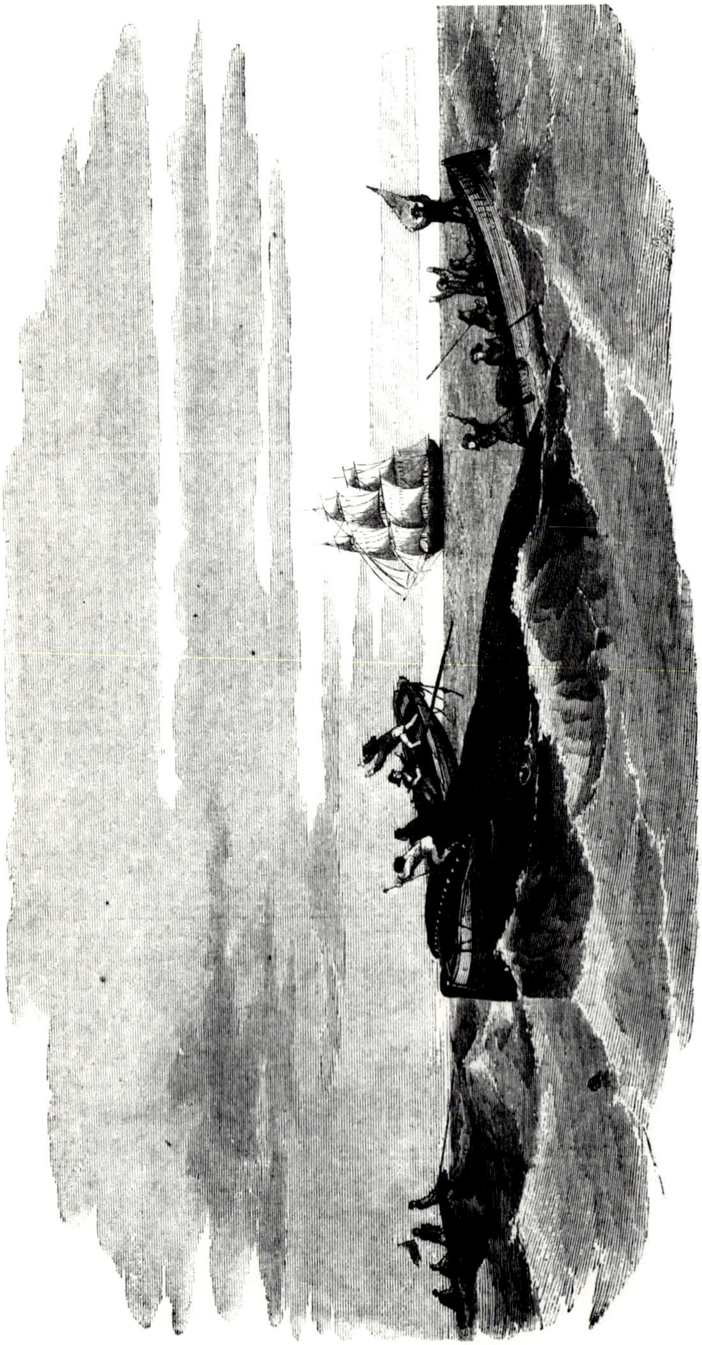

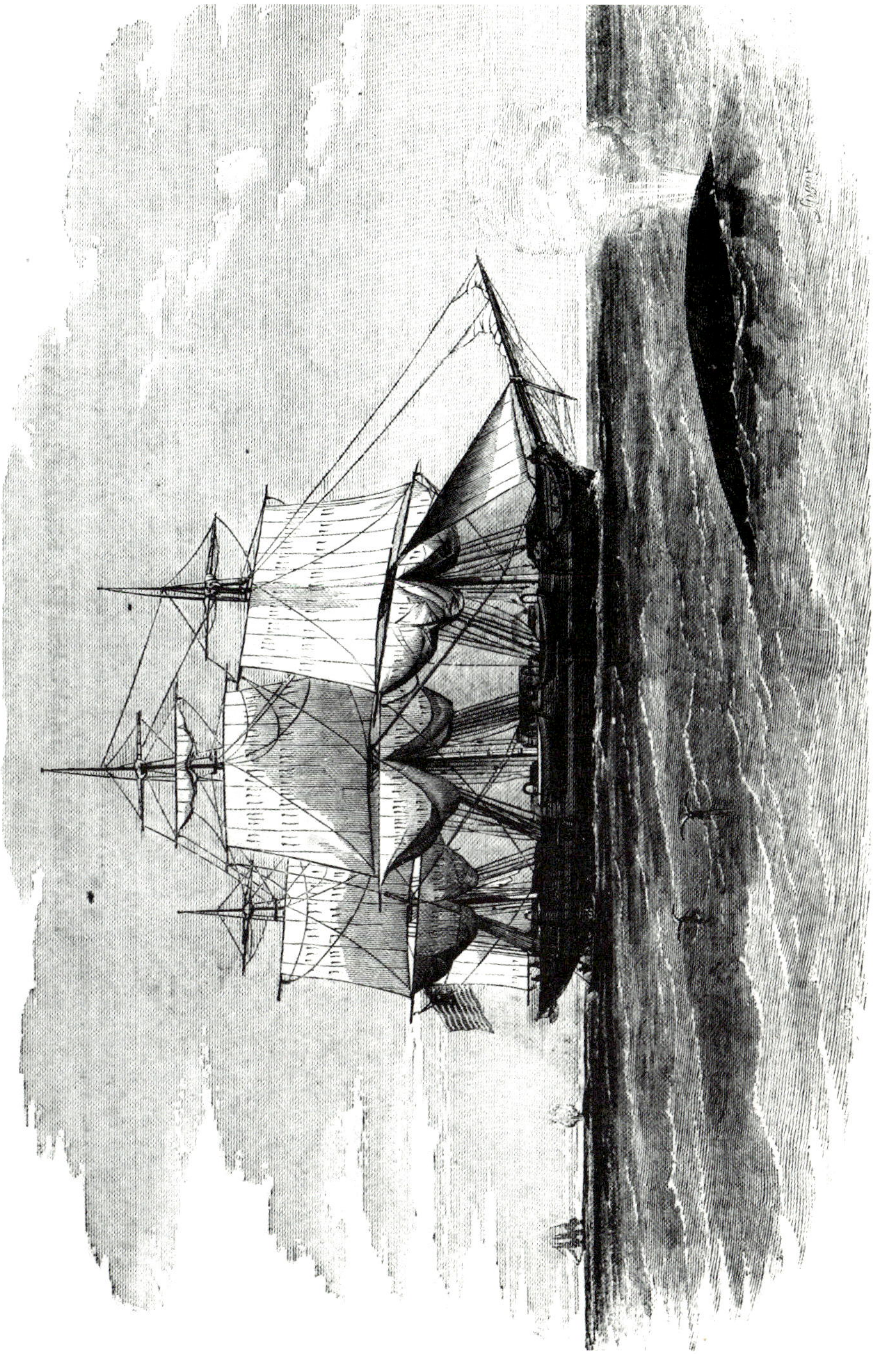

OLD SALTS, 1906
Surviving Cold Spring Harbor whalemen (left to right) George Barrett, George Mahan, Harvey Gardiner, John Douglas, and John Waters.

The people of Sydney, Australia, were full of sympathy when the survivors of the *Meridian* eventually arrived there. Several of the passengers and leading citizens started a collection for Captain Ludlow and his crew, with a gold medal being prepared for the master, his first mate, Jerimiah Eldredge, and seaman Charles Snow of the *Meridian*. In addition, silver medals were struck and engraved for each member of the *Monmouth*'s crew. Captain Ludlow also was to receive a testimonial of £300, the first mate £50, and Charles Snow £25. Lengthy testimonial letters were prepared for each of the three men.

Years later John Henry Rogers, who had been a seaman aboard the *Monmouth,* turned to peddling newspapers on a Brooklyn, New York, street corner. Known affectionately by everyone as "Pop," Rogers somehow managed to keep happy now that he was ashore, after spending much of his early life at sea. The old whaler was always proud of his part in the *Meridian* rescue. He was never without his silver medal from the citizens of Sydney, and said that he would not sell it ever, even for bread.

Ludlow arrived home in the *Monmouth* on May 3, 1854, and in January of the following year received two gold medals—one from the Royal Institution for the Preservation of Lives from Shipwreck and the other from the British Government—and an engraved gold chronometer, as some mark "of the signal courage and humanity displayed by him." The presentation took place at the office of the Customs Collector in New York and was attended by a number of minor dignitaries. In honor of the occasion the British Consul was authorized to distribute 100 guineas among the crew of the *Monmouth*. Captain Ludlow followed the sea for about two more years, then retired to his native Bridgehampton, Long Island, where he died in 1870.

8

Ship Ashore!

THE LITERATURE of whaling is replete with tales of shipwreck and disaster at sea. Herman Melville's classic *Moby Dick* describes the strange loss of the whaleship *Pequod* to a great White Whale. This, of course, is fiction, but three American whalers really were wrecked by sperm whales: the *Essex* of Nantucket, which was rammed twice by a bold and ugly eighty-five footer in 1820; the *Ann Alexander* of New Bedford was attacked and sunk by a vicious sperm whale in 1851; and the *Kathleen,* also from the latter port, which, in 1902, was struck and sunk by a terrified and confused whale her boats had been pursuing. Then, there were losses year after year by pack ice, fire, grounding, collision and even from hulls being eaten away by the devastating shipworm. And some ships just disappeared, never to report again. During the zenith of the whaling era, it was not unusual for a dozen or more ships of the whaling fleet to be posted missing at the end of a season. Cold Spring sailors were no strangers to these perils, as there are several surviving stories of danger and narrow ecapes.

The Cold Spring ship *Sheffield* had a fabulous season in the Bering Strait during the summer of 1850, taking some 3,000 barrels of oil and 45,000 pounds of bone. It was cut short, however, when her windlass broke and she was forced to return to Honolulu. On the passage back her crew had a most hair-raising experience in which they missed "sure and instant death to all of us by a distance of only 100 ft." Let Captain Thomas Roys, who commanded that voyage, tell the tale himself:

I was running to go through a passage among the Fox islands not very wide. Stormy and foggy, gale of wind. Our position was such that to heave the ship to for better weather was almost certain destruction. We missed the channel and ran into a horseshoe in the land and found ourselves suddenly close upon the rocks.... to tack or wear ship was alike impossible. The sea dashed up the perpendicular rocks for more than a hundred feet high. . . .

All was done that man could do to save the ship with every man at his post; two men at the helm. Some are weeping, some are praying, some in sullen silence look upon the all exciting scene and calmly wait the stroke of death at this critical moment.

The gale increases. The tremendous weight of the sale is making the ship groan throughout her extreme length. The sea is breaking over her, throwing the spray upon her topsails and wetting down the men at her helm. Her leerails under water. No word is spoken, for the proud ship is laboring with destiny and with fearful speed. She staggers on, bearing all on board to safety or instant death. Onward she drives, until only one wave is between us and the rocky bottom, barely at a distance of about a hundred feet.

Then the memories of years go flying through the brain, the cheek turns pale, the heart beats thick and the boldest hold their breath. In another moment she is free and a shout of joy resounds through the ship. The rocks are passed and orders to reduce sail are obeyed with alacrity and she runs in safety over the sea....

The Cold Spring whalers *Richmond* and *Edgar,* when placed in very similar situations, were much less fortunate, for they were both totally wrecked in northern waters. The wreck of the *Richmond* was extremely significant in a maritime sense, not only in itself but as well for the subsequent litigation regarding ownership of her salvaged cargo, which was argued all the way to the United States Supreme Court. The Court, in a landmark decision in the field of Admiralty Law, ruled in favor of the *Richmond*'s owners, stating that a salvor is entitled to a reasonable fee, according to circumstance, but not at any fixed or arbitrary rate. The decision went far beyond the scope of the original suit, because for centuries previously common law had provided that a fixed proportion, generally from a third to half of the value of the wreck and its cargo, was assigned to the salvors, according to the risks involved.

Captain Philander Winters, an "East End" Long Islander, took *Richmond* on her second whaling voyage out of Cold Spring for the Pacific with a crew of 32 men on July 21, 1846. Winters was a well-seasoned whaleman, having first sailed before the mast when just a lad, later filling the billets of cooper, boatsteerer, mate and master with three year's experience, before commanding the *Richmond*.

Richmond cleared Honolulu for the last time in November 1848, then headed for the Western Pacific and the Japan Sea, where she took four whales. She left the Sea of Japan in company of the Sag Harbor whalers *Elizabeth Frith* and *Washington*. The *Elizabeth Frith* sailed with *Richmond* throughout the season, with the crews gamming constantly between ships. By coincidence, the captain of the *Elizabeth Frith* was Philander Winters' older brother, Jonas. He had taken command of the *Elizabeth Frith* in the summer of 1847, sailing under the house flag of Post & Sherry of Sag Harbor on a cruise to the Japan Sea and the Arctic Ocean. He took with him two of their brothers, Charles, who had signed on as the cooper and Silas, as a boatsteerer and steward.

After leaving the Japan Sea, *Richmond* sailed along the coast of Kamchatka up toward the Bering Strait. The whaling was excellent there, especially in the Gulf of Anadir, where in a week she took six whales, which yielded some 1,200 barrels of oil. She then sailed northward, right into the Bering Strait, where the whales were "tame" and easily caught. *Richmond*'s new first mate, Charles H. Reeves, knew this fresh whaling ground well, having sailed there the previous season in the Sag Harbor whaler *Superior* on her epic voyage into the Arctic Ocean. *Richmond* took 10 fairly good sized whales there, and the 14 total she had taken that season produced between 2,300 to 2,400 barrels of oil, bringing the total quantity of "takings" on board to approximately 3,600 barrels of oil and 24,000 pounds of bone. On July 29, when the boat crews had just caught their last whale, the officers believed the *Richmond* had taken more whales than any other ship on the ground. They were able to accomplish this because there were three trypots aboard *Richmond* instead of the customary two.

Captain Winters needed just one more whale to fill *Richmond,* and everyone aboard was becoming especially anxious to finish, since dangerous pack ice would be arriving in 20 days or so. On August 2 the crew was still boiling and had some blubber left on deck and in the hatch from the whale which they had taken on the 29th. About noon, the ship was running west-southwest in a thick fog on a port tack. After dinner, Captain Winters told the first mate to relieve the watch, which he did, asking the captain if he should wear ship. Winters said no, telling the mate to let her go on the same tack until 6:00 P.M. Reeves later claimed that he openly disagreed with the captain, saying that he "thought it was impossible for the ship to go until that time; I had sounded [bottom], and told him there was but 18 fathom of water." Winters, he claimed, chose to ignore the warnings, remarking that, "if she would not go to that time, to let her go to hell."

This decision was extremely foolish, considering there was fog so thick that the lookout could only see a few ships' lengths in any direction. Sure enough, *Richmond* struck a reef or ledge about half a mile offshore between half past two and three o'clock that afternoon. She hit bottom several times, and on the third time, the rudder was driven clear up through the transom, locking it hard to starboard. The crew, however, was able to respond quickly, hauling all the sails hard aback, somehow managing to get her off the rocky reef on a heading to the northward. They immediately trimmed the after sails to counteract the rudder, which was now impossible to move. In addition, *Richmond* was taking water fast.

Having no helm, the crippled ship began to drift along the land, until she finally grounded between two rock ledges broadside to shore, about a mile from where she originally struck. The crew tried vainly to back her off, first clewing up the sails, then rolling eight casks of oil overboard to lighten ship. They pulled the bungs of over a dozen more to let some of the oil run out, and when the deck hands finally started the pumps, there were three to four feet of water in the holds. The captain ordered a boat crew to take a light stream anchor out from the starboard bow, and then tried to kedge her off with the capstan. It was all to no avail, for *Richmond* was hard ashore. Taking no chances that the ship should somehow float clear, Captain Winters left the stream anchor out and ran out the port bow anchor as an added precaution.

The crew left the ship about 6:00 that evening with the nautical instruments, some bedding, small stores, crockery, sails for tents, what clothes they had handy, and some provisions, and headed for the shore, which was about half a mile away. There was a high bank directly opposite the wreck, so the men had to row a few miles to the northward, around a point, where they found a protected landing place with a good sandy beach. Here they were, stranded in Siberia, on the tip of Chukchi Penninsula, roughly 1,000 miles from civilization and 27,000 miles from home port. Fortunately, some Eskimo natives were living nearby in whaleskin huts. They were friendly, and although communication was difficult even in sign language, the natives proved very helpful in getting some bread, molasses, flour, meat, sails and nails from the wreck. In addition to what had been brought ashore, the Eskimos provided the sailors with reindeer meat and fresh salmon.

The nights can be very short in this strange part of the world. There were only four hours of darkness at that time of the year, enabling the *Richmond*'s men to work almost continually between the ship and the beach. A few days after the grounding, Captain Winters took an axe and went out to the wreck, where he cut away the mizzen mast to try to ease the ship. He had decided to leave the cargo on board, since there was nothing to do with the oil and bone so far from civilization. There was actually little need for concern, since this was an excellent whaling area and there were a number of whaleships nearby, which could probably come in and take the stranded sailors off when the fog finally lifted. During this time, however, the crew was troubled by a persistent fire, started by the tryworks, which they had forgotten to "shut down" after the wreck. It was finally extinguished only after the entire works and the caboose were torn down.

The crew of the *Richmond* lost sight of the *Elizabeth Frith* a short time before the wreck, and it was not until the fog cleared on August 5 that she was seen again. The crew of the *Elizabeth Frith* had just finished trying out two whales, and they were ready to lower the boats and pursue some more. They still needed about 650 barrels to fill the ship, and this spot seemed ideal, for there were plenty of spouts in every direction. Suddenly, someone spotted a whaleboat sailing from the shore, heading directly for the ship. As the craft drew closer, Captain Jonas Winters realized from her paint that she belonged to the *Richmond* and William Sayre, the second mate, had charge. As the boat reached the ship, Captain Winters shouted down, asking what was the matter. "The ship is ashore," Sayre yelled back. "Don't you see her?" he said excitedly, pointing towards the wreck, which was still afire with sails fluttering in the breeze. "Is there anyone lost?" Winters asked, also inquiring if the ship was intact. Sayre replied that everyone was safe and the ship had not gone to pieces, but was full of water. When he came aboard, Sayre told Captain Winters that if the *Elizabeth Frith* had not come in that morning, the *Richmond*'s people were going to put out to sea in the boats and search for a ship.

Shortly afterward, another boat, with Captain Philander Winters and Charles Reeves, the first mate, left the shore. It is said that when the *Richmond*'s captain came aboard the *Elizabeth Frith,* he shook hands with his brother, broke down and cried, then headed straight for the privacy of the cabin. Philander Winters and his first mate were very anxious to get off, and he asked his brother to take himself and his men aboard, allegedly saying that the *Elizabeth Frith* need not whale any more that season, since there was plenty of oil which they could take. Jonas Winters supposedly objected, saying it would be illegal to remove the oil without buying it.

Leaving his captain aboard the *Elizabeth Frith,* Reeves cast off for the New Bedford whaler *Junior,* at anchor some distance to the south. When he was alongside, he told Captain Silas Tinkham of the *Richmond*'s predicament. The mate then returned to the camp ashore for the night, but on the following day brought his gear and made his home aboard the *Junior.* Meanwhile, Captain Tinkham brought his ship in closer and then went aboard the *Elizabeth Frith,* where he offered to take half of the crew with him, provided they took the other half. If another ship hove into sight he proposed that they should all divide the crew equally among them.

On the morning of the 6th, the *Elizabeth Frith* anchored about a mile from the wreck, and after breakfast a working party, equipped with axes, crowbars and similar gear, was sent aboard to see what could be salvaged. Arriving at the *Richmond,* the boat crew found the decks a mess, covered with casks, rigging, staves and blubber. During the next few days, men from the *Elizabeth Frith* and *Richmond,* working together, managed to haul out between 250 and 350 barrels of oil and the bone of approximately four whales' heads. That night, *Junior* came in and anchored about a mile from the wreck.

The following day, Reeves pulled some 15 to 20 miles out to the Sag Harbor ship *Panama,* which also was trying out blubber. Learning of the disaster, Captain Frederick M. Hallock brought his ship in and anchored about nine miles from the wreck. Previously, Captain Tinkham of the *Junior* had agreed to take part of the *Richmond*'s oil, "provided it was put up and sold at auction." Captain Jonas Winters of the *Elizabeth Frith* agreed, so his brother had a notice posted on the mainmasts of *Junior* and *Elizabeth Frith* and on the wreck itself. It read:

> Notifycashion. This is to sertify that the ship Richmond and cargo is to be sold at publick ockshion to the hiest bidder, without resurve, August 8th, 1849.

The auction commenced promptly at 8:00 A.M. on the 8th, with the four captains, several officers and a few boat crews present. John P. Carr, the first mate of the *Junior,* was the auctioneer. The first lot of oil and a proportionate amount of bone went to Jonas Winters of the *Elizabeth Frith* for $1 per barrel, and he was allowed to take as much as he wanted. The next was knocked down to Captain Tinkham of the *Junior* at 75 cents per barrel, while the last, also at 75 cents per barrel was struck off to Captain Hallock of the *Panama.* Quite a bargain this was, considering that whale oil was averaging about 40 cents per gallon, or some $12.60 per barrel, back home. While there was no limit as to what each captain could take, from a practical standpoint they could only salvage enough to fill their individual ships. The *Richmond* was auctioned off where she lay. Jonas Winters bid $1 for the hulk, but Captain Tinkham took her for a mere $5. No money changed hands, for payment was to be made when they all arrived at Hawaii. The auctioneer kept only a record of the prices, and there was no formal accounting of the quantities of oil and bone which were taken and no bills of sale.

After the auction, each of the three ships' crews stationed themselves at a hatch and commenced getting the oil out of the wreck. This was none too easy a task, for first they had to saw the deck beams to get working room and then, using tackles secured to the masts, and cant hooks to fasten to the heads, they managed to haul the barrels out and raft them to the waiting ships. It was far from pleasant, working in holds full of dirty water, gurry and oil, with stoven oil casks, staves, cask heads, stanchions, pieces of deck beams and blubber floating around.

The *Elizabeth Frith* took between 600 and 900 barrels of oil and roughly 6,000 pounds of bone. The *Junior* took some 700 to 900 barrels and a proportionate amount of bone, as well as the starboard anchor and both cables. The *Panama* hauled in from 600 to 700 barrels and about 3,000 pounds of bone. There is no way of knowing the exact amounts, since no formal records, but only some scribbled pencil notes, were kept and the oil and bone were mixed indiscriminately with each ship's own cargo.

Elizabeth Frith finished loading to capacity on August 12. Actually she was so cramped that her crew had to heave overboard sails, water casks, barrels, shooks and 1,200 pounds of bread. The *Panama,* which remained until August 16, had to throw about $500 worth of shooks and bread over the side. *Richmond's* two chronometers, two or three compasses and a barometer and medicine chest were taken aboard the *Elizabeth Frith*. William Sayre, *Richmond*'s second mate, took his boat crew aboard the *Panama,* while Reeves and William Cherry, the third mate, took their crews in the *Junior,* which stayed a few days after the others had left, for there were still about 800 to 1,000 barrels of oil which had not been stove in. When *Junior* finished and put to sea, *Richmond* was keeled over with the tide ebbing and flowing through her bones.

During the voyage to Hawaii, Captain Philander Winters became very ill and subsequently died on September 13 from what appears to have been a stroke, since it was said that "his misfortune so wrought upon him as to occasion the impairing of his mind and the use of his limbs." He was buried at sea. *Elizabeth Frith* arrived at Honolulu on September 2 with 13 of the *Richmond*'s survivors, while *Junior* arrived there on September 29 with the first and second mates and 11 seamen.

On April 20, 1850, Charles Reeves, *Richmond*'s first mate, landed at New Bedford in the whaler *Lagoda* and headed straight for Cold Spring, where he met with John H. Jones, the second mate, William Sayre, who arrived on March 25 in the *Panama,* and William Cherry, the third mate, who had reached New Bedford on April 4 in the *Montreal*. After each mate told his version of the wreck, the subsequent auction and the circumstances of the sale, Jones asked them if they thought he should sue to recover *Richmond*'s oil and bone. The mates felt that he should institute legal action, so Jones decided to meet with his lawyers and solicit their opinions.

The attorneys advised Jones that he had grounds for a legal action, so on May 23, 1850, the owners of the *Richmond* filed in the United States Court for the Southern District of New York. Basically, they asked that the ownership of the "cargo, materials and furniture of the ship," including that which had already been sold, be affirmed to them, subject "only to such fair and reasonable amount of salvage and freight, or either of them, as may be just . . ." and determined by the Court.

The original case involved only the owners of the *Elizabeth Frith* and *Panama,* but not the *Junior*. The Cold Spring owners' witnesses, Charles Reeves and William Cherry, gave very contradictory depositions, which were obviously influenced and embellished by their desire to get the full lays originally due to them. Both men staunchly insisted that the sale prices were established by the respective captains before the auction was commenced. The owners' attorneys refuted the authority of Captain Philander Winters to sell his cargo, and insisted that it still belonged to them. They did agree, however, on the basis of the evidence, that the rescue ships were entitled to salvage fees, and that the court should determine the amount of the award. In addition, the lawyers maintained that since the owners of the rescue ships could not prove that a valid sale had actually taken place, the service rendered was essentially salvage.

But the Sag Harbor people wove a skillful defense, using liberal testimony of officers from the *Elizabeth Frith, Panama* and *Junior,* who unanimously asserted that the sale was consummated under extreme necessity to save the cargo and was for the good of all concerned. Their attorneys insisted that Captain Philander Winters, as the owners' agent, had the authority to sell the cargo. Several "disinterested" whaling captains testified that they probably would have acted as the masters of the *Elizabeth Frith, Panama* and *Junior* had, if placed in similar circumstances. It was all very smooth and convincing.

Not surprisingly, the Court ruled in favor of the owners of *Elizabeth Frith* and *Panama.* Basing his decision on precedent, Judge Andrew T. Judson decreed that whenever there was a moral obligation, extreme peril or extreme necessity, the master had the power to sell his vessel, and under similar circumstances, the cargo as well, provided that it belonged to the same owners as the ship. Judge Judson could see no evidence of collusion between the two Winters brothers. He believed that the sale of the *Richmond*'s oil was apparently *bona fide,* was for the good of all concerned, and was made under conditions of extreme necessity. The judge excused the fact that no money changed hands, because when Philander Winters died there was no one else authorized to receive payment when everyone reached Hawaii. Although there was no bill of sale, the oil was in fact delivered and a memorandum of the auction was produced in court. "An actual sale and delivery of personal goods, orally, will carry the title as well as a bill of sale," Judge Judson noted.

The court did not believe that there was any salvage service involved. Salvage, the judge insisted, is the compensation made to persons who assist in saving a ship or its cargo from impending peril or actual loss. In giving up the opportunity of taking more whales, which everyone admitted were abundant, Judge Judson said that he could not believe that the masters would have passed up the chance to fill their ships in a few days for a transaction which might be subject to litigation when they returned home. They had, he asserted, taken the oil by an expressed agreement at a stipulated price. Thus, the libel was dismissed on June 29, 1852.

The *Richmond*'s owners were not satisfied with the decision, so they appealed to the Circuit Court. The lower court ruling was subsequently reversed on September 21, 1855, and the sale declared void. The salvors, however, in consideration of their efforts, were entitled to a moiety, or one half, of the net proceeds of the *Richmond*'s oil which was brought back by the *Elizabeth Frith* and *Panama*. In addition, the owners of the *Richmond* were entitled to seven percent interest, from the date of sale on the New York market, on their half of the proceeds.

The Sag Harbor owners refused to abide by the appeal, so they brought the case to the United States Supreme Court, which agreed to hear the complaints in 1856. On January 28, 1857, in a decree important in terms of Admiralty Law as it applies to salvage, the Court stated that while a master had the power to sell both his ship and cargo in cases of absolute necessity, the exercise of this authority had to be closely scrutinized by the courts, lest it be abused. The Court, however, believed this rule had no application to a wreck in a distant ocean, where the property is deserted, or about to become so, and the person who has it in his power to save the crew and cargo prefers to drive a bargain with the master as the price of safety. Then it struck down the old concept that the reward for saving derelict property should be fixed at "not more than a half or less than a third of the property saved." The reward, the justices maintained, should be made according to the circumstances of each particular case.

The specific case at hand, involving the *Richmond,* was held to be one of derelict, since the transfer of the cargo required no great exertions or long delay. "The contrivance of an auction sale under such circumstances . . . where there is no market, no money, no competition . . . is a transaction which had no characteristic of a valid contract." The court allowed that the salvors were entitled to a moiety at the first port of entry, which was Hawaii, and to an additional freight allowance for transporting the owners' half to a better market at the home port.

Following the Supreme Court decision, the owners of the *Richmond* received $10,200 from the *Elizabeth Frith* and *Panama*. After they had paid all court costs, legal fees and expenses, there was only $7,500, which was apportioned $5,000 to the owners and $2,500 for the *Richmond*'s crew. This was a considerable loss to all, considering that the cargo of approximately 3,600 barrels of oil and 24,000 pounds of bone probably would have brought more than $40,000 on the New York market had the ship completed her voyage.

Supported by the Supreme Court ruling, the *Richmond*'s owners, or their heirs, sued in the United States District Court in New York, on April 26, 1858, for the portion of the cargo brought in by the *Junior*. Samuel R. Betts, the district court judge, citing the precedents just established in the Supreme Court, decided that the owners were again entitled to a moiety of the proceeds of all cargo and materials obtained by the *Junior,* after the deduction of freight from Hawaii to New Bedford. The owners of the *Richmond* finally had won their rightful property, but more important, had helped establish a precedent which would protect derelict ships against unreasonable salvors, radically changing the law of salvage and placing the determination of settlement in these cases where it belongs, in the courts.

The Cold Spring ship *Edgar* cleared for her only whaling voyage on November 25, 1852, with a crew of 28 men. Her skipper, Samuel B. Pierson, 37, had previously sailed as master of the *Splendid* in 1848, and did well for the owners, having brought in 3,400 barrels of whale oil and 38,000 pounds of bone in March 1851. Pierson's son Charles, 18, signed on as a greenhand for the voyage and his brothers, Theodore, 30, and Elihu, 21, joined as first mate and green boatsteerer. The crew, half of them recruited in the captain's home town of Bridgehampton, Long Island, were mostly young men in their late teens or early twenties, and included an Indian, named Nathaniel P. Cuffee, who sailed as a boatheader.

Edgar finally arrived at Honolulu on May 11, 1853, after a rambling outbound passage of almost six months. While at Hawaii, Captain Pierson signed on four Kanakas and then sailed to the Arctic for the summer whaling season. When she arrived back at Honolulu in early December, *Edgar* had taken 350 barrels of whale oil and some 5,000 pounds of bone. Pierson cruised again until February, and then returned to Honolulu to recruit. He sailed on the North Pacific grounds during the summer of 1854. This season was much more successful than the previous, for he took about 1,500 barrels. *Edgar* returned to Honolulu in November and shipped home 195 bundles of whalebone, weighing 21,236 pounds and 119 casks of oil. Twelve of the men were promoted, probably as the result of the successful season.

SHIP ASHORE!

This ship, incidentally, had one of the most stable crews, in terms of turnover, of any ship to sail from Cold Spring. Captain Pierson decided to work the Eastern Pacific during late winter 1854-1855, and put into Guam during the latter part of February with 80 barrels of sperm whale oil on board. *Edgar* sailed in March, probably for the Japan Sea, then the Sea of Okhotsk, for the summer season.

Whaling was very poor in the Arctic during the 1855 season on account of tempestuous weather, which claimed at least four or five whalers, including the *King Fisher* and *Enterprise* of New Bedford, which were lost on the same day, May 13, 1855, in the Kuril Islands; the *Jefferson* of New London, which was lost on Sakhalin Island off the Russian Coast; and then *Edgar* was wrecked on St. Jona Island, now known as Ostrov Iony, in the Sea of Okhotsk on the morning of June 5th.

On June 3, *Edgar's* men had sighted nothing but ice and seals; then on the following day a thick fog set in and the ship became trapped in the ice to the south of St. Jona for about five hours. She had worked free by the 5th and was tacking along the edge of the ice with 15 to 20 ships in sight, either lying to or boiling. At 4:00 A.M. thick fog set in once again, but the island was still a good distance away—NNW about 12 miles. As a precaution the crew soon took in sail and began to wait out the fog. Suddenly, the island appeared out of the gloom, barely two or three ships' lengths away. All hands were called, the sails were lowered and the helmsman put the wheel over hard, hoping she could wear around the land. It was futile, for the ship quickly swung before the wind and struck rather gently, her bowsprit jutting out over the rocks. *Edgar* lay there for perhaps 20 minutes, then swung clear, only to hit again about two ships' lengths away to the leeward, where she remained hard and fast.

The crew then lowered all boats and lay off in sight of the ship until daylight, when they went back aboard after some difficulty, and found that she fortunately had not bilged. The fog lifted a bit and when a sail was sighted south of the island, Captain Pierson dispatched the second mate to her to report that *Edgar* had been grounded and to ask for help. The ship proved to be the New Bedford whaler *Roman II,* Captain Seth M. Blackmer, who then came on board and offered all the assistance in his power. *Edgar* had about 1,600 barrels of whale oil and 7,050 pounds of bone on board, and Captain Blackmer was able to salvage the bone, which was on deck, and 48½ barrels of whale oil. In keeping with the current salvage custom, he took half of both for himself. *Edgar's* barometer, chronometer, sextant and charts were taken aboard *Roman II* for safekeeping. Later that day the fog lifted, the weather cleared, and the *Jireh Swift,* also of New Bedford, spotted *Roman II* standing by the wreck. Captain William Earl of the *Jireh Swift* rowed over and took a few small items—about 600 fathoms of towline, a boat and nine of *Edgar's* men, including a boatheader, boatsteerer and cooper. One of the men was seriously injured, having fallen from aloft, while cutting away the spars soon after the ship struck.

At sundown, however, an immense pack of ice, towering 20 feet high, came in from the south and drove the three ships off to the northward. Meanwhile, two boat crews each from the *Roman II* and the *Charles Carrol* had been left at the wreck to save what they could. The working party was able to burn a hole in the ship's side and get out 700 barrels of oil, which was rafted near the wreck, but the ice carried the casks away and broke them up. Captain Pierson and part of his crew had been taken aboard the *Roman II* soon after the grounding and were unable to reach their ship again until the ice cleared eight days later. When they returned they found barrels of pork and oil floating in the frigid waters and the *Edgar,* which had been burned, covered by eight feet of water.

Three other ships, which were standing off the island, were able to get out more of the oil and raft it out, but only with great difficulty, for the men were constantly exposed to the elements and soaked to the skin, frequently having to jump into the freezing waters to free the rafts from obstructions. The *Alice* of Cold Spring salvaged about 120 barrels, the *Cicero* of New Bedford, about 130 barrels, and the *Young Phoenix,* of the same port, another 80 barrels. In all, 380 barrels of oil and 3,525 pounds of bone were saved. *Roman II* bought 764 gallons (25½ barrels) of whale oil from Captain Pierson, and the bone was shipped back to New York in November when Captain Pierson arrived at Honolulu. *Edgar's* crew, taking only the clothes on their backs, were divided between the *Roman II, Charles Carrol* and *Jireh Swift* for the voyage back to Hawaii.

Captain Pierson, carrying the *Edgar's* papers which had been saved from the wreck, boarded the *Frances Palmer* for San Francisco on December 1. When he subsequently arrived at Cold Spring, the owners, while disappointed by the wreck of one of their ships, could not complain too bitterly of financial loss. The *Edgar* and her outfits were valued for underwriting purposes at $24,000 and were insured for three-quarters of that amount. The oil and bone salvaged from *Edgar* netted $3,600 and the owners received $15,700 in insurance settlements. Considering the value of previous shipments of oil and bone from Honolulu, plus the proceeds from the salvaged cargo and insurance, against the value of the ship, her outfits and two and one-half years' cost and maintenance, the owners at worst broke even and probably made a slight profit on the only whaling voyage of the *Edgar!*

The Joneses had confidence in Captain Pierson, in spite of his losing the *Edgar,* for they gave him command of the *Splendid* in 1856. Pierson had difficulties with his officers and made a poor voyage this time out. A boatheader, who had signed on, claiming to have been cheated out of $50 by Captain Pierson, wrote an anonymous letter to John H. Jones and his sons from Honolulu in November 1857, in which he bitterly attacked the captain, alleging that all Pierson did aboard *Splendid* was "Gam Gam and get drunk and keep gameing," or else ". . . curse his hard luck and the Joneses. . . ." It was strong stuff. He also said that ". . . it is well known here how the Ship Edgar was lost. The truth has not all been told at home." There was plenty of ale, champagne, rum, brandy and liquor aboard, he claimed, along with sacks of nuts. ". . . in port it is rum and squaws and at sea it is rum and cards. . . ." and so it went. Pity was that Captain Pierson had to wait two and one-half years before he got home to defend himself.

The Cold Spring whaling industry was now entering into its period of decline. Twenty percent of the fleet was wrecked on distant shores, and two ships, the *Nathaniel P. Tallmadge* and *Tuscarora,* had been sold. By the time Walter R. Jones died on April 6, 1855, interest in the fleet was already waning. In a half-dozen years Cold Spring whaling would be no more.

9

Some Distinguished Cold Spring Whalers

THE VAST majority of the approximately 2,500 men who sailed in the Cold Spring whale fishery remain anonymous, but some were just colorful enough to be remembered. While most of these men were nonresidents, a few were Cold Spring natives, and names such as Jones, Rogers, Titus, Gardiner, Lisle, Mitchell, Douglas, Van Cott, Brush and Valentine appear on the old shipping lists. The Barrett brothers, surely, were the best known of the lot. In 1851 George W. Barrett sailed as a foremast hand in the *Alice*. When he returned home he joined the *Sheffield* as first mate on her last voyage out of Cold Spring from 1854 through 1859.

George Barrett's brother, DeWitt, made his first whaling voyage under Captain Richard Smith of the *Splendid* in 1851. They had been out 7 months and 10 days without a drop of oil, when they suddenly had a turn of luck in the Bering Strait. Some pretty strenuous days and nights followed, and the whole ship was so stacked with blubber that the crew had to put into shore to try it all out. In just two months *Splendid* took 2,000 barrels of oil and the entire voyage was completed within 18 months. From 1854 to 1859 DeWitt sailed with his brother George in the *Sheffield*.

The youngest Barrett brother, Freeman, was also called to the sea. On a fateful voyage he got a limb caught in a line which was bent on to a harpooned whale and was dragged overboard and carried down several fathoms. Struggling feverishly to work loose, Freeman succeeded in cutting the line with his sheath knife, then rose to the surface and was rescued. He never really recuperated from the experience, however, and died soon after reaching home.

Like most Cold Spring youngsters of those days, George Mahan started work at an early age. He was employed in the brickyards of Joshua Jones, but when he saw the trim whaleship *Nathaniel P. Tallmadge* lying at anchor in Cold Spring Harbor, Mahan "used to look at her and long to go to sea." He finally had his wish when he was 20 years old and shipped before the mast with Captain William Hedges in the *Nathaniel P. Tallmadge* on the 1843 voyage bound for the Southern Ocean in quest for whales. The first whale fastened to off the Crozet ground was a huge fellow, and he sounded, boat and all, after being harpooned. Fortunately, George Mahan and his crewmates were all strong swimmers and were saved after some frantic minutes in the cold waters.

While at New Zealand, Mahan took sick and was put ashore in care of the United States Consul at the Bay of Islands while his ship sailed off to the North West Coast grounds off Alaska. As soon as he was well enough, Mahan took a look around, and realized that he was stranded a long way from home and it was "too far to float with a life preserver." So, the homesick whaler decided to ship aboard a vessel which took him to New Bedford, and from there worked his way back home to Cold Spring.

Manuel Enos was probably Cold Spring's best known whaler. A bear of a man, almost 6 feet tall and weighing about 225 pounds, he originally shipped aboard a Sag Harbor whaleship at Fayal in his native Azore Islands. "Big Manuel" subsequently made his way to Cold Spring, where he shipped in *Huntsville* for her 1849 and 1851 voyages. Upon returning in 1854 he signed on the *Sheffield* under Captain H. J. Green, joining several local men, including George and DeWitt Barrett, Warren Gardiner, John Lisle and William McGarr, the ship's carpenter. A hard worker, Big Manuel was advanced to boatsteerer.

Manuel Enos was well-liked in Cold Spring, especially by the children, who were fascinated by his thrilling tales of adventure. He loved to take a child on each knee and show them coins and strange shells he had collected in his distant travels. Big Manuel grew to like the little village so much that he decided to settle there and marry Susan Brush, a girl from a fine local family. Big Manuel—surely at the urgings of his young wife—decided to stay ashore. He owned a kid leather factory and store for a time, but it failed, so he had to return to the only trade he ever really knew, whaling. Manuel bade farewell to his wife and little daughter, Melna, and went to New Bedford in search of a ship.

At New Bedford, Enos signed on for a first mate's lay in the *Java* under Captain Edward B. Phinney. The ship cleared on September 6, 1860, and when she returned in May 1864 *Java* had made a particularly "greasy" voyage, having 1,292 barrels of sperm oil, 284 barrels of whale oil and 1,700 pounds of bone on board. Big Manuel received a bonus of $250, and the ship's agents, G. & M. Howland, had such confidence in him that he was promoted to captain for the 1864 voyage and offered a $1,000 bonus if he could bring in $100,000 worth of bone and oil in two seasons. "Captain Manuel" worked the Pacific and Indian Ocean grounds, then made a run up to the Arctic.

Captain Manuel returned to New Bedford on April 25, 1869, and found the owners very pleased with his accomplishments. He then left for home, where he found that his little Melna had died and another baby, Ella Nora, had been born shortly after he had left for sea. When the ship's accounts were all settled, the *Java*'s agents sent a letter to Captain Manuel, stating that the ship had cleared $96,200, just $3,800 short of the amount needed for the $1,000 bonus! But the owners were so pleased with the voyage, they decided to send Captain Manuel the money anyway.

Utilizing his new-found wealth, Captain Manuel built a fine house on Cold Spring Harbor's Main Street. He then purchased his own vessel and turned to the coastwise trade. Once again he failed in a strange business, so he returned to whaling, signing on as mate of the New Bedford whaler *John & Winthrop*. Later, in 1882, he became captain of the *Matilda Sears* out of Talcahuano, Chile. Captain Manuel never returned home again, and was presumed lost at sea with all hands.

Two Cold Spring captains, Hiram Hedges and Jeremiah Mulford, were residents of East Hampton, Long Island. Captain "Jerry" Mulford was a kindly, yet proud and impetuous man, who often suffered from poor digestion acquired from years of living at sea. After he retired, unlike most of his profession, Captain Jerry was reluctant to discuss his past seagoing experiences with his family. There was one incident his wife said that he wanted to forget, and it happened while returning home from his last whaling voyage in 1848.

The story began after two years of whaling off South America, when some of the *Nathaniel P. Tallmadge*'s crew became homesick. Captain Jerry took the bunch of 'lubbers into port and promptly shipped them back. In their place, he signed on a few Portuguese sailors, and it soon became apparent that they did not understand Captain Jerry or his language, nor did he understand theirs.

After cruising in Alaskan waters, the *Nathaniel P. Tallmadge* touched at Hawaii, before running for the "Horn" and then home. She was only a few days out of Honolulu, when Sam Stratton, the carpenter, and the first mate noticed that a big Portuguese sailor was evidently trying to incite the others to mutiny. "We three officers must keep in sight of each other," Sam told Captain Jerry, because "trouble's brewing among the men." How right he was, for within twenty-four hours, the ringleader had seized a marlinspike and struck the captain on the head. Fortunately the mutiny was aborted when the big sailor was placed in handcuffs. In spite of his head wound, Captain Jerry took charge and had a large cask brought up on deck. Then he ordered some staves removed, placed the man upright in the barrel, headed it up and took him back to Honolulu in this very novel brig!

It would have been difficult for any man, whether he sailed as master, an officer or even before the mast, to forget the days he spent on a Cold Spring ship, or any whaler for that matter. Conditions were grim, to say the least, and the air was filled with either boredom in the extreme or electrifying excitement during which each man risked his life many times in the course of a voyage. There are a few old and yellowed newspaper accounts of meetings of Cold Spring whalers who chanced to cross paths years later. Like all good shipmates, they would sit down, reach for a bottle of porter or ale, and "gam" for hours, reliving again those hair-raising experiences of some two or three decades previous.

10

Most Daring Whaleman Of Them All

THOMAS WELCOME ROYS was no ordinary Cold Spring whaling captain. Without question he was one of the greatest American whalemen. Born far from tidewater in Wayne County, New York, about 1816, he began his career at the age of 17 as a greenhand in the Sag Harbor whaler *Hudson*. Roys rose to master in just eight years, and from that time on his inventiveness, pluck and daring were unrivaled by any man in the industry. In 1848, for instance, he was the first American whaleman to sail through the Bering Strait deep into the Arctic Ocean, where whales were more numerous than on any other ground anyone had ever known. Roys returned a hero and soon took command of the Cold Spring whaler *Sheffield*, distinguishing himself again by landing one of the largest cargoes in the port's history. Thomas Roys had a probing, scientific mind and made significant contributions to contemporary cetacean knowledge. He was respected and consulted by the leading oceanographers and biologists of his day. In addition, Roys was a successful inventor and holder of a number of patents for improved harpoons and other whaling devices. Roys conducted many of his experiments in Iceland, and in Norway he is regarded as the father of modern whaling. In his declining years he returned to North America and attempted steam whaling—rather unsuccessfully—off the Canadian west coast. Thereafter his fortunes waned. Roys died in obscurity, forgotten save for a paragraph or two in whaling histories.

While captain of the Sag Harbor ship *Josephine* from 1843-1846, Roys first learned of an unusual whale that was taken in the North

Pacific in 1845 by Captain Soldering of the Danish ship *Neptune.* This animal was different from any Roys had ever seen and he immediately thought that there must be more father north. Because he had only poor charts aboard, Roys feared to venture beyond the Bering Strait, where these strange whales most surely resorted. Fortunately, while in Petropavlovsk-Kamchatskiy, Roys was able to obtain a set of good Russian charts for $100 and learned from a naval officer that there were plenty of whales to the north.

As soon as he arrived home, Roys pored over narratives of polar exploration, all of which confirmed his previous beliefs, but did not give any indication whether it was possible to catch this mysterious new species. The lucky break came in July 1847, when Roys took command of the Sag Harbor bark *Superior,* a scant 275 tons. He dared not broach the idea of sailing into the Arctic Ocean with the ship's conservative owners and he also knew that he would have to use the greatest diplomacy in getting a crew up there. Besides, the owners had given specific orders to work the South Atlantic grounds, fully expecting the ship to return with a full cargo in about eight months. Roys worked the Crozet Island grounds at first, but only took seven small whales. When it appeared that the ship would not be full in the allocated time, the crew became very discontented. Roys then proposed that Captain Freeman H. Smith of the Cold Spring whaler *Huntsville* and others join him in sailing into the Pacific, secretly, of course, setting his mind's course for the Arctic. But all of them refused and even ridiculed the idea. *Superior* arrived at Hobart, Tasmania, with just 120 barrels of whale oil on March 7, 1848. It was too early to head for the Arctic, so Roys sailed for a short, unsuccessful cruise in the South Seas. Returning to Hobart, he decided to sell the oil and refit for a year's cruise. He wrote the owners that he was going through the Bering Strait, "and if no tidings came from me they would know where I went." *Superior* cleared port on May 20.

Captain Roys cut a course northward, but since it was too early to enter the Arctic Ocean, because of ice, he worked the area below the Bering Strait from the Aleutians to the Siberian coast. When *Superior* reached 60° N. latitude, the chief officer became very alarmed and conveyed his fears to the entire crew. After all, these seas had previously been visited only by explorers, who told vivid tales of threat by ice and natives. Everyone complained so the captain was forced to return to the 57th parallel where they worked for the month of June. Taking no nonsense, Roys told his officers that he fully intended to go through the Strait. They were terrified and declared that they never expected to see home again.

In mid-July *Superior* passed through the Bering Strait into waters no whaler had ever known. Just as they entered the forbidding passage, the crew's admonitions seemed realized when seven native umiaks, each bearing approximately forty men, crossed from the Alaskan to Siberian coasts. The captain wisely decided not to signal them, since his ship was only partially armed.

On first entering the Arctic the going was rough, with the ship encountering thick fog and pelting rain. In fact, the weather was so bad it appeared they were lost. The stories Roys had read were true, however, for soon he saw the mysterious whales he sought. They looked, he wrote, ". . . as I fancied a polar whale should. . . . But my officers declared they never saw such a . . . animal before and were not inclined to meddle with the new fangled monster. . . ." The first whale was taken by Roys himself at midnight.

The whales in this new and strange place, the captain noted, were easily caught, almost "tame," and entirely different from any which he or his men had ever taken. They took three distinct kinds: right whales, yielding 160 to 170 barrels; "bowheads," "bamheads" or "steeple tops," as they were called by the whalers on account of a bow-like mouth and a pronounced forehead; and the small, white beluga whale. The bowhead, of course, was the whale which Roys had been seeking.

While Roys concerned himself with filling the ship, the officers and crew were living in hourly expectation of some unforeseen calamity. They were practically beside themselves with fear and the captain actually believed that they would have attempted mutiny, if it would have succeeded and gotten them away from the Arctic Sea. Actually, their fears were ill-grounded, for generally conditions were ideal. They saw no ice and it was so pleasant they were able to work in just light clothing. Then, the ocean proved so shallow, *Superior* lay at anchor most of the time in from fourteen to thirty-five fathoms.

Superior cruised from continent to continent up to the 70th parallel. When the crew finished cutting in on August 22, they had filled the ship with 1,800 barrels of oil in just 35 days, a feat which normally required two seasons, at least, to accomplish. The ship called at Honolulu on October 4 and Roys received a broad welcome. She arrived at Sag Harbor on May 5, 1849, after 21 months and 21 days around the world.

Despite warnings of thick fog, powerful currents and the dangerous ice, coupled with poor charts and the paucity of navigational information for the area, whalers flocked to the new ground. Roys had put new life into a dying industry, for in 1849, *Superior* was followed by a fleet of 154 ships, which took 206,850 barrels of whale oil and 2,481,600 pounds of bone. The following year, 145 ships cleared and returned with 243,680 barrels of oil and 3,654,000 pounds of bone. The Arctic whale fishery proved popular for decades!

Roys' daring and success were the talk of the entire industry. *Superior* had no sooner arrived from the epic voyage than he was approached by Walter Restored Jones, who had been very favorably impressed. Jones and his friends decided to act promptly and engaged Roys for a voyage in the *Sheffield* to whale the "Icy Sea." Roys sailed out of New York Harbor on August 17, 1849. He had been handicapped by *Superior*'s size during his previous Arctic venture, so welcomed the opportunity to command a ship fully three times larger.

Before setting out for the Arctic, *Sheffield* called at San Francisco with a cargo of prefabricated houses and lumber for the "Forty-Niners." There were rugged times on the voyage out when a vicious mutiny was narrowly averted. But she reached 'Frisco safely, where the crew found a number of their Sag Harbor cronies, grumbling that the pickings were poor. Captain H. Green was hard hit, having lost almost $3,000 in the gold fields. But the brother of one of the boatsteerers was lucky, having cleared $600 in just seven weeks. Success when it did strike was usually short-lived. One of the crewmen told how he made his way up 'Frisco's muddy hills where he found saloons with gaming tables claimed to have been better attended than the churches. It was a wild scene, what with hundreds of prospectors, fresh from the gold fields, packed into a single room and clustered around some ten gambling tables. The stakes ran from a dollar to as high as $20,000. Those not playing the tables took turns at the bar, cards or just gratifying their curiosity by spectating.

Sheffield cleared for Honolulu on April 2, 1850, with Roys and the crew boasting that they expected to take 5,000 barrels of oil in 90 days. One local, suspecting a bit of exaggeration in their vow, mused, "I hope they will do it but sha'nt be disappointed if they don't." Three weeks later *Sheffield* came to anchor in Honolulu harbor to recruit for an Arctic whaling season. She sailed on May 1. As a precaution against native attacks, the ship had been fitted out with a large cannon, 4 swivel guns and 24 muskets, but there could be no protection from the ice and shipwreck.

The ship reached the Arctic just in time for the summer season. Whaling was excellent that year, but the weather was especially brutal. In late August, while lying at anchor, a fierce gale ripped into *Sheffield*. While getting underway to beat off shore, the windlass gave away, forcing Roys to leave the grounds much earlier than he had intended. He put into Honolulu for repairs and decided to work the warmer waters of the Pacific during the winter. But again *Sheffield* was buffeted by a storm, no doubt a fall typhoon, and was forced to limp into Hong Kong. Despite the weather, it had been a very good voyage so far.

Unfortunately, the 1851 Arctic season was not nearly as successful, but the 1852 season was so outstanding that Captain Roys had to leave the grounds early for want of casks. The owners back in Cold Spring must have been very pleased, for he had taken 7,200 barrels of oil and over 100,000 pounds of bone for them after just 36 months out. Not satisfied himself, Roys took another 1,600 barrels before heading for home via the South Pacific and New Zealand. *Sheffield* finally arrived at New York—after almost four and a half years—on January 23, 1854, with a full cargo. Roys was surely one of the best captains in the industry!

By his own admission, whaling and its natural history were the only interests of Thomas Roys' life from first taking to the sea at age 17. He rather modestly conceded that, "My knowledge is merely practiced not scientific as I came to Sea too young to acquire any thing more of an education than is taught in the common school and I have neglected and forgotten the most of that and there has been no one at sea . . . to teach me, every thing gives place upon a whale voyage to the obtaining of Oil, consequently there is little else attended to." Yet, Captain Roys' observations and opinions were sought by the leading oceanographers of the day. In fact, he considered Lieutenant Matthew F. Maury, the father of modern oceanography, as one of his close friends.

The first contact between Maury and Roys began in October 1849. Maury, then director of the National Observatory, was soliciting information from leading clipper captains, naval officers and whaling masters, to be used to prepare charts and sailing directions. Maury was particularly interested in "the habits and places of resort of the whale." In the course of his research, he wrote to a number of whalers, including Roys and the captains of the Cold Spring ships *Alice* and *Huntsville*.

Roys replied to Maury in part, that, 'I am writing a book, with all the knowledge I possess, giving a particular description of all kinds of whales, with all my opinions, &c., which I will forward unto you upon my return to the States. . . . I can only say," he continued, "that I heartily rejoice that we have one man in our Government who will condescend to take notice of a business, the annual income of which is millions, and at the present time has broken down all competition of other nations."

Early in 1854, just after arriving home in *Sheffield*, Roys forwarded his manuscript "Descriptions of Whales" to Lieutenant Maury. The little book was a masterpiece, considering the improbable source, for it listed, illustrated and described 18 species of whales, plus covered the various northern Pacific grounds and surrounding shores in detail.

A perceptive observer, Roys realized as early as 1854 that the whale populations on the old grounds were being depleted faster than the animals' reproduction rate would allow. He suggested that if the government really wanted to aid and foster the whaling industry, it should send some small research ships, carrying one or two men "acquainted with every kind of whale," to the south latitudes above Antarctica in search of new grounds. He felt rather strongly that "there is not the slightest ground to doubt their discoveries will be of great importance to the whale fishery. . . ."

Charles M. Scammon, the famous natural historian of the West Coast, interviewed Thomas Roys during the 1870s and drew heavily on his remarks for the Arctic whale section of his *Marine Mammals*. In fact, there is a full page illustration of the so-called "Roys whale" in the book. This bowhead subspecies, originally called a "bunchback" by Roys, is distinct in that it has a small hump on its spine. The Latin name for the animal, *Balaena mysticetus Roysii*, honors America's only whaleman-oceanographer.

During the winter of 1854-55, Roys went to England, where he examined the ice protection of the Hudson Bay ships and consulted with renowned English polar whaler William Scoresby. He returned to New London, Connecticut, where he met with Benjamin Brown's sons, the managing owners of the ship *Hannibal*, and suggested how to prepare her for the first American whaling voyage to the Greenland Sea. The Browns decided to ignore Roys' recommendations and had only reinforced the ship from two to three feet above the waterline to two feet below, using some heavy uprights to protect the bow. "She was expeced to navigate heavy ice," he complained, and "in vain I remonstrated against this folly. I was obliged to go as she was, or give up my cherished expedition and look a good natural fool. I consented to go in hopes a favourable season might enable me to gain Cumberland Inlet and obtain a cargo."

Hannibal sailed on May 21, 1855, and when Captain Roys arrived at Davis Strait, between Greenland and Baffin Island, he found the ice too thick, precluding the slightest hope of getting *Hannibal* into Cumberland Inlet. Roys was beside himself, for the owners had cautioned that if the ship was lost in the ice, he would be responsible. They would rather have sacrificed the voyage than the vessel.

Roys remained off Davis Strait until the latter part of September, then cut a course for Lapland, intending to spend the winter near Iceland. The sulphur bottom whale, long considered too swift and dangerous, was never taken by the old-time whalers prior to this time.[1] Using a Bowen's bomb gun he killed a sulphur bottom which yielded only about 30 barrels. Roys believed that if he had a better weapon it would be possible to have filled *Hannibal* with sulphur bottom oil. But the weather was against him too; the ship was buffeted by a heavy gale, causing the upper works to leak badly. *Hannibal* was forced to put into Lorient, France, for repairs.

While in *Sheffield,* Captain Roys had given some thought to using a device similar to the bomb lance to kill sulphur bottoms. During the repair of the *Hannibal* at Lorient, he ordered two paired rifles, to be used on the next cruise. Roys informed the Browns of his idea, and one of them promptly arrived in Europe, asking him to end the voyage. The request was not unreasonable, for Roys had only 36 barrels of oil to show for an entire season on this novel ground. The ship would probably have done infinitely better in the Pacific. Roys refused to return home, so he was quickly relieved of command.

Returning to New York, Roys was astonished to find that a claim had been filed with the insurers of the *Hannibal* because of his "insanity!" The owners used the letter Roys had written concerning his whale gun for evidence, because it stated, "if my gun fired as I

---

[1] Later, while working off Iceland, Roys took an astounding 147-ton animal. It was 95 feet long, had a girth of 39 feet and yielded 110 barrels of oil and 800 pounds of baleen.

expected, a cargo of oil could be obtained which would be neither Humpback, Right Whale or Sperm." How absurd, they thought, since these were the only commercially practical species at the time. Roys wanted to resolve the matter quickly, so he suggested that one of the Browns meet him before the underwriters. The owners refused, so the claim was promptly abandoned.

In 1856, not long after returning from France, Roys persuaded two friends to join him in purchasing the tiny 174-ton brig *Wm. F. Safford* and outfitting her for Spitsbergen whaling. The guns which he had ordered in France were lost in the S.S. *Pacific,* so Roys approached C. C. Brand of Norwich, Connecticut—the inventor of the bomb lance—and since there was not enough time to fabricate duplicates, had him build a weapon capable of firing a three pound bomb —the heaviest which could be shot from a shoulder gun. If he found no right whales off the northwest coast of Russia in the vicinity of Novaya Zemlya, Roys intended to use the new device to kill finback, sulphur bottom, blue and bottle-nosed whales, all of which had not been previously caught by American whalers. The *Wm. F. Safford* sailed from Sag Harbor on May 5. When Roys finally reached Novaya Zemlya he could find no right whales, but saw vast numbers of blues, "the largest and most powerful of created beings . . . about 100 feet long and 14 feet diameter," as well as a great many finback, sulphur bottom, humpback and bottle-nosed whales.

Roys fired his gun many times off Novaya Zemlya, but managed to kill only two humpbacks and a huge, 92-foot long blue. He saved 44 barrels of the blue's oil, but lost the rest. A great many animals spouted blood, but did not die immediately. Roys deduced that the weapon was not powerful enough, so he headed for England, hoping to make improvements. He applied for, but was refused, a patent for his device, because it utilized the polygonal rifling system which had been recently patented by Joseph Whitworth, a well-known British engineer. By sheer accident Roys was introduced to Whitworth, whom he asked to make another whale gun.

Roys continued with his voyage, but on the first firing of one of the Whitworth guns he met with an unfortunate tragedy:

> We sailed from Queenstown bound south and when in the Bay of Biscay I took up one of my guns to try the explosion under water. Standing on the main hatch, I fired the fuse, ignited the powder in the shell, and it exploded, blowing up the gun and sending me backward about 8 feet. I did not fall. Looking around me, I inquired who was

hurt. There was no reply. I then saw lying upon the deck a finger with a ring upon it which I knew, and looking, I saw my left hand was gone to the wrist, but for the moment it had given no pain only a sensation of numbness. Walking into the cabin I sat down and had it amputated [by the mate, Rogers Bishop] as well as we could with razors, and we now steered for Oporto but taking a severe gale of wind, the rig was hove to under bare poles and so heavy was the sea, there was no possibility of keeping the arm still and it had to be again amputated to save my life.

When we reached about 30 miles from Oporto, [which took about 17 days], it became calm. I lowered away my boat and pulled for Oporto but they would not let me land as there was no ship in sight. I sent for the American consul . . . who was out of town, and when he arrived I was allowed to land, and the arm was amputated. Before the operation, they told me I could not live but I did not believe them. It was amputated, and in two months I was in England.

When Roys reached Oporto in December 1856 he placed the ship in command of Rogers Bishop, directing the mate to put into Liverpool the following April. Recovering quickly, Roys reached Manchester, England, where he blew up another gun before finding an acceptable fuse. Then he began waiting, rather impatiently, for the *Wm. F. Safford* to come in. When she failed to arrive by June, Roys began to fear that she had been lost. He was almost ready to quit for home, when Joseph Whitworth offered to secure another ship, the *Pacific,* which was being fitted out for whaling when the *Wm. F. Safford* finally came lagging in.

Roys decided to leave the *Wm. F. Safford* under Rogers Bishop, and accompany him in the *Pacific*. But again the experiments with the bomb gun failed. Shells where were capable of piercing wrought iron and oak ricocheted off the tough hide of a whale. Roys returned to England again, where he had the front of the shell squared off, so they could be fired directly through the water and still puncture the whales' skin.

While in England, Roys developed an entirely new gun, based on the Congreve rocket—long a weapon of the British military—which was capable of firing a line and harpoon-bomb from the shoulder, much in the same manner as a modern bazooka. Roys left *Pacific* in the docks at Liverpool and in October 1857 sailed in *Wm. F. Safford* as far as South Georgia. He caught nothing there, finding instead that his rocket gun still needed numerous improvements.

He then cut a course for Iceland, where he killed two blue whales, but both sunk. Roys' luck turned when he took a 95 and a 35 footer.

He sailed for Lisbon, got new shells and powder for the rocket and then beat toward the West Indies, where he discovered that the harpoon bombs were still not satisfactory. In April, Roys put into Jamaica, obtained new weapons, and then set sail for Iceland, where the two new guns blew up on the first day.

When he finally returned to England, Roys found a group of dissatisfied creditors and was forced to surrender the *Wm. F. Safford* to the Admiralty Court for sale. Fortunately some friends, Joseph Whitworth prominent among them, paid most of his bills, saving him from the embarrassment and indignities of a British debtors' prison. Roys then refitted the *Pacific* for another cruise. This time he had a hundred of his new harpoons on board.

Roys' ability to cope with failure was amazing, for when he came up off St. Vincent and fired at a sulphur bottom, the harpoon again went right through and exploded, permitting the whale to swim off with boats and lines. It was simple to correct this, however, for all he did was insert a strong iron bar into the shaft of the harpoon, preventing it from penetrating more that 5½ feet into the blubber and flesh before bursting.

This final modification proved perfect, for every whale struck thereafter was killed. The gun, which weighed 16 pounds and was balanced on a man's shoulder, was capable of firing from 60 to 100 feet away. It fired—without recoil—a 16-, 18- or 21-pound explosive, barbed harpoon attached to a four inch line. The bomb detonated just eight seconds after entering the whale. The only remaining problem was quite serious. The whales almost invariably sunk after being killed. Even though the harpoons held fast, Roys was able to retrieve only three animals. After a number of them were lost in deeper waters, the pods seemed to sense the slaughter and moved off.

Although the owners of the *Pacific* had lost about $25,000 in his last venture, they agreed to let Roys keep the ship, provided he fit her out again on his own. He was deeply indebted to them, having lost about $25,000 of his own, but somehow he hoped to raise the $5,000 needed to fit out for another voyage.

Roys' experiments had been successful in so far as they proved that additional species of whales could be taken, since there was at long last enough power to kill them. He could finally say that ". . . it is now all over with the poor whales. The weapon cleaves them like fate, making an internal wound about 10 feet in diameter closing at once every artery of life."

Recounting the trials leading to the perfection of his rocket gun, Roys was the picture of optimism:

> ... For 5 long weary years I have pursued this object sacrificing my property my limbs my friendships and my loves, yet the knowledge that my operations must greatly benefit mankind is a solace that my hand is not lost in vain. As for my property, that will come back again if my patent is secured to me....

After four years of research and experimentation, Roys was awarded his first British patent for improved rocket guns in 1859. When he returned to the United States during the fall of 1860 he immediately went to New Bedford to demonstrate his gun, finding little interest because it cost $25. He then went to Washington, where he received a patent for his gun on January 22, 1861.

Roys' American patent of June 3, 1862, secured an improved version of the rocket harpoon. "The nature of my invention," he wrote, "consists in providing a rocket-harpoon with a cavity loaded or filled with an explosive compound, which will be fired as a bomb by the burning of the rocket, and greatly increase the destructive action of the weapon." Although Roys was able to perfect the rocket gun and harpoon rather early in his experiments, many of the whales he shot sunk and were not able to be recovered. Roys found the answer to the problem in his patented "whale compensator," a mechanical contrivance for raising sunken whales.

Around 1861, Roys purchased a small interest in the Excelsior Fireworks factory in downtown New York City, where fireworks, flares, fuses and torpedoes were manufactured on a large scale. Undoubtedly he had been drawn to the plant's proprietor, Gustavus Adolphus Lilliendahl, by the young man's prominence in the pyrotechnic field.

In June 1862 Roys sold a quarter interest in his rocket gun, whale compensator and an improved propeller patent to Lilliendahl. For the next five years they worked together in perfecting the rocket powered harpoon. Pyrotechnic knowledge was crucial, for poor propellant and fuse powder mixtures had dogged Roys' experiments for years. The initial fruit of their joint efforts was a patent issued in 1862 for an improved war rocket. In ensuing years Roys and Lilliendahl received additional patents in Norway, Holland and France for their inventions.

In 1863 Roys and Lilliendahl embarked on a series of experiments which are said to have been the demarcation point between the old and modern whaling methods. Sailing from New York in the bark *Reindeer,* they arrived in Iceland by mid-summer. The following summer they took 20 whales.

In November 1864 Roys secured residency and fishing rights in Iceland. He returned there in 1865 in the *Reindeer* and the Danish steamer *Visionary,* which had been fitted out in Scotland, and established a shore station at Seydhisfjördhur, on the eastern coast. *Reindeer* served as the processing ship at the station, while *Visionary* was the whale catcher. When an animal was killed and captured, the little steamer took it in tow and brought the carcass alongside the station ship to be tried out. But the 1865 expedition had bad luck. Of the some 40 whales killed, only 16 to 20 were actually taken. The rocket harpoons continued to malfunction, but Lilliendahl arrived in August and was able to repair some of them. In the late fall the *Visionary* ran on the rocks and was wrecked, so the expedition returned to Dundee, Scotland.

Roys—wanting to keep the mechanics of his guns secret—entrusted the actual handling of them to his brother Samuel and half-brothers William Henry, John and Andrew. William Henry, Samuel and Andrew were so sure of the venture they became citizens of Iceland. One of them even brought his wife along, but the crew objected that a woman would bring them bad luck.

Lilliendahl and Roys decided to prepare still another offensive, this time in the steamers *Steypireydur,* Captain Samuel Roys; *Vigilant,* Captain William Henry Roys; and *Sileno,* Captain Andrew Roys. The whole expedition had a very cosmopolitan flavor. It was a joint enterprise manned by Americans, Swedes, Danes and Icelanders. The ships were British owned, yet flew the Danish flag. The whales were processed aboard the *Steypireydur* and *Vigilant,* which were equipped with costly experimental hydraulic press/steam kettles supposed to be capable of extracting oil from both blubber and bone. Unfortunately, the kettles failed and the catches had to be processed at the land station. There were other failures that season. Some 80 out of 100 harpoons were found to be defective and had to be reworked at the station.

The Roys-Lilliendahl rocket, while not a revolutionary concept, attracted considerable attention in the European scientific community. Congreve rockets had been used for over half a century, most notably —to Americans—by the British in the War of 1812. Sir William Congreve, himself, as early as 1821, had proposed using rocket guns to kill whales, and his basic idea was so similar to the Americans', it is presumed that Roys studied the former's work at the Royal Arsenal at Woolwich. In 1866 Svend Foyn, the inventor of the modern-day harpoon gun, sailed to Iceland to witness the American experiments. He went away with a wealth of information, but firmly believed that the rocket method was more costly than his own.

Foyn was particularly impressed with the Americans' catching methods. The three steamers sailed out to sea, each towing two 33-foot whaleboats. As soon as a spouter was spotted, the seven-man crews took to the boats in pursuit. When within firing range, the harpooner would take aim and launch the rocket harpoon. If the whale died instantly, the boat came alongside and signaled the steamer to take the catch into the station. The steamers were equipped with stout winches and Roys' "whale compensator," a combination of elastic rubber straps, which was used to raise whales which sunk.

By September 1866, 40 whales were taken. Mostly blues, but also some finbacks and humpbacks, they produced 2,300 to 2,400 barrels of oil. But expenses were outrunning profits and the business was losing money. Roys pulled out and sold his interests to Lilliendahl and Henderson, Anderson & Company of Liverpool. Lilliendahl remained for another year with *Steypireydur* and *Vigilant,* catching 36 whales; but it was hopeless. The business went bankrupt and the shore station was liquidated at auction. The first American attempt at modern whaling had failed. Beaten, Lilliendahl went home to his fireworks business, politics and finally building and promoting railroads in Mexico. He died there in 1907.

From the outset there was considerable interest in the American expedition to Iceland. In December 1865 Captain O. C. Hammer founded the Danish Fishery Company to foster the whaling and fishing industry in Iceland. Before actually commencing operations, he contacted Thomas Roys, who agreed that one of the Danish firm's ships could study his methods. John Roys and three other Americans, gunners and boatmen, instructed the Danes. In exchange for this service, Hammer agreed to purchase a large number of rocket harpoons. The Danes were impressed, so they bought a little whaling steamer, which was fittingly christened *Thomas Roys.* Captain Hammer arrived in the ship in May 1866 and established a whaling station, with Captain Roys, at Hafnarfjördur on the southwest coast of Iceland. The Americans soon parted company, however, when Hammer accused them of sabotaging his expedition. The Danish effort and a Dutch expedition both failed after only a few years.

Svend Foyn succeeded with his harpoon cannon where Roys left off. Actually both guns were equally effective, since 140 whales were taken from 1865 to 1872 with Roys' method and 143 by that of Foyn, which was, however, unquestionably more economical. But it is only fair to realize that Foyn profited by the mistakes of Roys and Lilliendahl, making sure to test his own gun on a much smaller scale before embarking on an all out attempt at modern whaling. Thus, in their small way, these two Americans made a solid contribution to the development of modern whaling.

When Captain Roys returned to New York City he began manufacturing "rocket harpoons, rocket shell harpoons, rocket shells, and whale raising compensators." This venture must have failed, for a year later Roys went to San Francisco to continue his experiments, then turned to whaling in steamers off British Columbia on the west coast of Canada.

He arrived at Victoria in late spring or early summer 1868, and found that several independent whaling expeditions were starting out. Roys, for himself, hoped to use rocket harpoons extensively. But again he was plagued by minor difficulties. Working quickly, because the humpbacks would soon be migrating south, the defects were again corrected and it was soon predicted that "certain annihilation awaits any of those deep sea monsters. . . ."

By September Captain Roys was ready for a two-month cruise. He cleared Victoria in the chartered steamer *Emma,* which had been fitted out for whaling with an 18-man crew. This time the improved rocket worked splendidly, for two whales, yielding 65 and 45 barrels, were taken the first week out. Unfortunately, the weather turned bad and coming in after a month out, Roys complained that he had only two and a half days clear enough to work. Even so, the local merchants were impressed with the venture, so much so that they decided to back Roys by incorporating and funding the Victoria Whaling Adventurers Company with a capital of $10,000.

In December Roys went to Honolulu where he hoped to sign on some experienced hands for another season. It took him only a few weeks to convince enough men that British Columbia offered excellent prospects as a new whaling ground. After all, it could be reasoned that there were plenty of humpbacks, sperms and sea elephants to be had just a few days out of Victoria, whereas a season's voyage from Honolulu was almost always a costly four to six month proposition.

Expenses too were lower in Victoria; casks were half the going price in San Francisco and oil and bone could be landed a lot closer to a good market than at Hawaii. British Columbia—it seemed—had everything to offer!

Arriving at Victoria in January 1869, Roys had a fine party of whalemen ready to go to work. By February they had *Emma* well fitted out with plenty of rocket harpoons, six guns, two whaleboats and gear. On March 23 she cleared for Barclay Sound to commence operations. Here, the expedition built a whaling station, where they erected buildings, a wharf, furnaces and trypots. Plenty of whales were sighted, but poor weather prevailed, and to make things worse the first whale they shot escaped and was later found and claimed by the coastal Indians. Roys temporarily abandoned the station and proceeded to Deep Bay above Nanaimo, his old whaling ground, until the weather cleared and he could return to Barclay Sound. Again he was unlucky, seeing only two whales, which eluded him. *Emma* headed for Nanaimo, then unsuccessfully pursued a large pod of whales sighted off the North West Coast.

On the return run, *Emma* broke her propeller. The merchants had had enough. They voted to dissolve the whaling company in June, selling the outfits at auction a few months later. Ironically, on the very day that Roys left the vicinity, a pod of a dozen whales swam right into Victoria harbor, with one of them actually running ashore, then floating off, ". . . as much as to say, come and catch me, if you can!"

Roys by this time was bound for Honolulu, where he hoped to try a turn at whaling in the Islands. He chartered the little schooner *Anne* there, then sailed for a bay near Lahaina, where he erected a shore station. After only a month out, *Anne* returned to Honolulu with 70 barrels of oil. Then, in April 1870, Captain Roys demonstrated his rocket harpoon to the Honolulu maritime community, probably to secure further backing for his expeditions. Everyone there was impressed, with some of the older mariners being heard to remark that it was one of the best whaling weapons they had ever seen.

Captain Rufus Calhoun, a wealthy shipowner from Washington Territory, who had brought Roys out to Hawaii in the packet brig *Byzantium* the summer previous, agreed to invest $8,000 in another expedition. Roys returned with him to Victoria, where *Byzantium* was fitted out to cruise Queen Charlotte Sound in the summer and the Gulf of Georgia in the fall. No expense was spared; tryworks were installed on deck and every contemporary whaling appliance was provided to insure a good catch. The following summer of 1871, *Byzantium* again cruised north as far as Gumshar, where her crew erected a shore station. The reports back from the grounds that year were excellent and by summer's end four whales were taken.

Roys seemed plagued by hard luck. At midnight on the 19th of October, *Byzantium* was wrecked in a southeast gale off Vancouver Island, and the 13 crewmen took to the boats with only the ship's barometer and some of their personal belongings. The following day they returned, but could find no evidence of the wreck. They therefore assumed that the ship had gone down with her cargo of 100 barrels of oil. Later, however, word was received that *Byzantium* had actually drifted off and the coastal Indians found her, cut the anchor chains and worked the ship out of sight, where they plundered anything they desired, including the sails and cabin furniture. The total loss was $15,000. The men found their way back to Victoria, where one man, the cooper, died of exposure. Captain Roys, dejected and disillusioned, bummed a passage on a lumber ship for San Francisco in November 1871.

Reaching San Francisco, Roys was broke both financially and spiritually. He had not seen his wife and family in years. Ann Eliza Green, his first spouse, had died—after only four years of marriage—in 1847 following the birth of their son Philander. Roys met his second wife, the former Marie Salliord, when he was refitting *Hannibal* in Lorient, France. An attractive woman, almost twenty years younger than he, she emigrated to America with him and settled in Peconic on the "North Fork" of Long Island, where she was an accomplished music teacher. Being away at sea so much, Roys had little time for Marie and their three children. Eventually she tired of being a "whaling widow," and some five or six years after arriving, shocked the community by eloping with one of Roys' former shipmates, said to have been a more handsome and favored man.

After his arrival in San Francisco, Roys' activities are unclear. He was surely broke, for in June 1872 he sold an eighth part of his patents to Hugh H. Lamont, a machinist in a local foundry, in exchange for some rocket guns, harpoons and accessories. In the fall of 1876, he turned up in San Diego, to join a ship. A few months later, however, he contracted yellow fever, was put ashore and was found wandering in the streets of the grubby little Mexican port of Mazatlan, sick, destitute and incoherent. He never recovered and died a week later—on January 27, 1877—of a stroke.

Ironically, the rocket harpoon began to be used successfully in the California and Alaska whale fisheries for some time after Roys' death. Roys rockets were a featured exhibit at the Great International Fisheries Exhibition of London in 1883. Gradually both his accomplishments and failures were forgotten, and as one obituary so aptly summarized Roys' life, it "goes to show that energy, pluck and ambition are not the sole elements of success."

11

The Long Voyage Comes To An End

Homecoming was a jubilant time, yet in some ways it was traumatic. Some men never returned at all, having given their lives to the industry, while others came back sick and weakened by strange, tropical illnesses, or, perhaps, maimed by the fury of a mad sperm whale. The long voyage from the last port of call was a period of psychological doldrums, trying both officers and crew to the limit of patience. There was plenty to keep the men busy though, and the mates made good use of this time to have bone cleaned and bunched, gear stowed away and the ship washed, cleaned and painted inside and out. When the ship was a day or two from port, a curious ritual was almost always performed. The tryworks, which represented hours of bone tiring, dirty work, was torn down and the brick and mortar heaved into the sea in a ceremony symbolizing the completion of another voyage.

Depending on the time of year, the amount of oil and bone on board and market conditions, the returning ships would either put in at Cold Spring or call first at New York to obtain the best price for the cargo, and to avoid the chance of encountering ice in Long Island Sound. The masters generally used the cross and spire of St. John's Church to pilot in safely past the "Middle Ground" and into the harbor. A gun which stood on Cannon Hill on the west side of the harbor opposite the steamboat wharf signaled the arrival of a whaleship. Nearby, a sharp-eyed youngster in the old Bungtown School would usually spot the whaler laden with oil and bone coming down through the harbor and then the rest of the boys, who should have been studying their lessons, all gazed out to watch the commotion and excitement as the ship came to anchor.

It was always a festive day in the village when a ship came in from a three or four year absence with husbands, brothers and lovers on board! Just about the whole town was at the wharf, and when the crewmen finally stepped ashore they jumped up and down, overjoyed to see their loved ones and to feel the ground beneath their feet once again. Just as soon as the sailors hit the tiny port, Cold Spring came to life. Numerous peculiar looking characters, speaking in a babel of languages, swaggered along Main Street, which was soon dubbed "Bedlam Street," rather appropriately, by the disgusted villagers. A number of Portuguese sailors and Pacific Island Kanakas stayed in the village for a time, living at the Stone Jug, a combination inn and saloon, where the proprietress, it is said, had the pleasant faculty of getting along with them. It was not at all uncommon during the height of the industry to find several Kanakas busily carving bone ornaments in front of the place. But the damp Long Island climate tended to deal harshly with these strangers, and one poor fellow, who died of "quick consumption," was buried in the woods by his friends.

J. Arthur Harris compared the return of a Cold Spring whaleman to that of a logger who went into camp with a roll of bills, or a miner who packed down from the diggings with his bag of gold dust, with the only difference being that the whaler strode ashore with his lay. "When these things happen," he wrote, "there is money for all who have aught to offer in return." Some men took to alcohol during the long dull voyages, and arrival in home port only tended to bring out the worst in them. The residents complained continually about drunken sailors, but, admittedly, there were a few rare occasions when crews did behave like gentlemen. This was so unusual, however, when the *Huntsville* arrived on June 28, 1847, the editor of the *Long Islander* was prompted to mention that, "What is remarkable in the arrival of this ship is, that she was manned by thirty-one men—all came on shore, and nearly one half left for their respective homes, sober and steady, within twenty-four hours after she arrived, and not one has been seen intoxicated." The parsons of the village were a persuasive lot and succeeded in inducing a number of sailors to sign the "pledge."

When the cargo of oil had been unloaded on lighters a specialist called the "gauger" came down and certified the amount and type of oil which had been brought in. Some was sold right on Long Island, but most of it was consigned to a major market such as New York City. Two Quakers, Amos and Samuel Willets, usually received the oil at New York. Their firm, Willets & Co., which dealt in marine hardware, was financial agent and part owner of a large number of whaling vessels, some 40 or 50 during their heyday, including the Cold Spring fleet. The Willets generally handled most of the ships' business for the owners, procuring supplies, honoring captains' drafts and selling oil and bone for the account of the owners.

Tallying the amounts remitted by the captains for "takings" which were sold overseas during the voyages, then adding the proceeds for oil and bone which was either shipped home or landed by the ships, Willets & Co. arrived at the gross receipts for a particular cruise. This hopefully was a substantial amount, and in some cases actually reached $50,000 to $60,000 or more for a single voyage. The crew's lays, starting with the captain's, the ship's outfit and expenses were then deducted from the gross. Before a seaman received his lay, however, deductions were made for advances he had received during the voyage, as well as items he had charged from the ship's slops chest. The crew's pay was generally the largest single expense for the whaling voyage, as witness a $33,700 payment to the men of the *Splendid* in May 1856. Individual shares might range from a cabin boy's meager pay of say $88, which Jo LePont of the *Huntsville* received in 1854, to the respectable sums, often running into thousands of dollars, that the captains took home. After several successive "greasy" voyages, a master could buy a farm and retire to the life of a country gentleman.

Some men did not come home with the ship, preferring to take their discharge at an outbound port so that they could get right back on the "grounds" again. This was particularly true after a poor voyage. In March 1850 Captain Edward Halsey, unable to find American or foreign seamen to take the *Monmouth* home from Honolulu, signed on five Kanakas for an advance of $20 and monthly wages of $16 for the trip. Halsey did this with some difficulty since the Governor, possibly fearing that natives might be exploited, was reluctant to let them leave. The American Consul interceded and secured permission only after promising that the Kanakas would be returned directly to the Islands without delay.

After the expenses had been deducted and paid, the remainder was divided among the owners of the ship as a dividend, the amount depending upon the number of shares each person held. In 1855 the owners of the *Sheffield,* as an example, received $16,000, which was divided on the basis of $125 for each 1/128th share of the vessel, while that same year the *Nathaniel P. Tallmadge* netted $27,953, providing a dividend of over $800 for each 1/32nd interest. The following list of the shareholders, and the number of shares they held, for the *Alice* in 1857, is typical:

Joshua Hall	2/16
Ship & Owners	2/16
W. R. Jones	3/16 & 1/128
D. S. Miller	2/16
John H. Jones	5/48
John D. Jones	1/24
Charles B. Moore	1/24
David Leavitt	1/16
Joseph S. Jones	1/128
Charles H. Jones	1/128
Charles Hewlett	1/128
Ebenezer Hale	2/16
Willets & Co.	1/32

The shares, as in this case, were generally divided into 8ths, 16ths, 24ths, 32nds, 48ths, 64ths, and 128ths.

The table on next page is based on a reconstructed set of accounting returns for the bark *Monmouth* from August 1851 to May 1854, using a shipping list with the crew's lays, records of the ship's take, currently prevailing prices for bone and oil, and a reasonably fair approximation of the value and distribution of the proceeds for the voyage.[1]

In 26 years of operation and 44 voyages Cold Spring whalers took over $1,500,000 worth of oil and bone. During 1851, the best year on record, the fleet grossed almost $250,000. Throughout this period some rather friendly competition prevailed between the various Long Island ports. Sag Harbor, of course, claimed the largest fleet by far, with Greenport, Cold Spring and New Suffolk tagging far behind.

Captain Thomas W. Roys, of course, made the best Cold Spring voyage in *Sheffield* from 1849 to 1854, having taken about 8,600 barrels of oil and over 115,000 pounds of bone, all worth almost $100,000. *Huntsville,* from 1849 to 1851, made the second best voyage, taking some 150 barrels of sperm whale oil, 3,350 barrels of whale oil and 64,065 pounds of bone, all of which was worth over $75,000 on the contemporary market.

---

[1] See Earle, Walter K. *Concerning the Whaling Museum at Cold Spring Harbor: and Also Something About Whales and Whaling.* Whaling Museum Society, Inc., Cold Spring Harbor, 1946, 1956 and 1961 edns.

WHALING BARK *Monmouth*
August 1851 through May 1854
(Rounded to nearest $50)

GROSS RECEIPTS:

345 bbls. sperm (10,350 gal. @ $1.50)	$15,550	
1,380 bbls. whale (41,400 gal. @ .55)	22,750	
11,700 lbs. bone (11,700 lbs. @ .32)	3,750	
TOTAL GROSS		$42,000

EXPENSES:

Crew's lays:

Captain	1/16		$2,600
First Mate	1/23		1,850
Second Mate	1/40		1,050
Boatsteerer/Cooper	1/40		1,050
Boatsteerer	1/80		500
Boatsteerer	1/80		500
Shipkeeper	1/75		550
Carpenter	1/100		400
Steward	1/105		400
Cook	1/120		350
Seamen (Experienced)	1/115	($365 x 7)	2,550
Seamen (Green)	1/170	(247 x 9)	2,200
Total Wages (26 men):			$14,000
Ship's Outfit (fitting out expense), est.:			10,000
Ship's Expenses (Provisions, repairs, payments to crew, etc. during voyage), est.:			5,000
TOTAL EXPENSES:			29,000

NET PROCEEDS: (To be divided among the owners after deducting agents' commissions)   13,000

In 1850 the Cold Spring whalers were doing unusually well on the newly opened Arctic grounds. Honolulu was a forest of masts that year, with some 100 whaleships, mostly American, in port at one particular time. The owners at Cold Spring were delighted by the reports from the fleet and a full accounting appeared in the *Long Islander* on January 10, 1851:

> Letters have been received by John H. Jones, Esq., the Agent of the whalers at Cold Spring, which gave very encouraging accounts of their success. The vessels are all full, or nearly so, and bound home, with the exception of the *Sheffield*....
>
> The following is a list of the vessels and cargoes:
>
> | | | | |
> |---|---|---|---|
> | *Huntsville* | 3,500 bbls oil | 50,000 lbs bone |
> | *Alice* | 2,800 do | 35,000 " |
> | *Sheffield* | 3,000 do | 42,000 " |
> | *Tuscarora* | 2,100 do | 28,000 " |
> | *Tallmadge* | 2,800 do | 40,000 " |
> | *Splendid* | 3,500 do | 48,000 " |
>
> The cargoes of the above ships at the present valuation is about $350,000. This is almost equal to digging gold in California.

The lure of California gold, of course, was strong competition throughout the period. Ironically, a man who bought passage in *Huntsville* from Honolulu to New York arrived in 1849 with $40,000 worth of gold from California, which was said to have been the largest amount brought from the gold regions up until that time. Honolulu, of course, was extremely dependent on "recruiting" whalers, and was overjoyed at the new found successes in the Arctic, which everyone hoped would help revive interest in the industry. With obvious bias, the Honolulu *Polynesian* editorialized:

> These may be called splendid voyages and as productive as the gold placers of California; and attended with much less risk to the moral and physical constitution than digging gold in the Sierra Nevada. Short voyages, with a full ship bound home, are rather pleasant circumstances for the whalemen, and a greater number never left this port than will sail this Fall [1850] in this category.

A "brisk and advancing" whalebone market in the fall of 1855 provided another boost to the lagging fishery and some Cold Spring ships supposedly sailed principally for bone, which was then in extraordinary demand for use in making ladies' hooped petticoats.

But even this was not enough to save Cold Spring whaling, which began to decline rapidly after that year. The causes for the ebb were several. Probably, lagging interest on the part of the owners might be singled out as the primary reason. Walter R. Jones, unquestionably one of the moving spirits of the whole venture, died in 1855, while John H. Jones, his equally enthusiastic counterpart at Cold Spring, was well on in years, passing away four years later at age 74. The stockholders, to be sure, were none too pleased with the partial failure of Willets &

Co. in November 1857. Apparently the agents were unable to meet a $16,000 dividend for *Huntsville*'s current voyage, so John H. Jones' son, John D., suggested that the owners settle for extended notes and property, lest they all be embarrassed when the crew came in and found that there was not enough money on hand to meet their lays.

The shipwrecks of *Richmond* and *Edgar* had their effects, too. In larger fleets, with as many as 50 ships or more, owners could "average" their losses, but in Cold Spring the wrecks of two ships in nine was plain disaster. The expensive and lengthy litigation regarding the ownership of the ill-fated *Richmond*'s cargo contributed little to continuing interest. Surprisingly, despite the increasingly widespread use of cheaper oils, such as fish oil from the menhaden, which was plentiful in the Long Island area, and kerosene, resulting from the discovery of petroleum in Pennsylvania in 1859, prices for whale products from 1859 to 1862 remained relatively stable, and actually rose substantially during the Civil War. The war, however, was a major blow to whaling, for soon after the outbreak of hostilities Confederate privateers, and later the famous raiders *Alabama* and *Shenandoah*, began to scour the seas in search of Yankee whalers. The conflict had another direct effect on the Cold Spring industry in that there had always been a shortage of good crewmen, especially after the discovery of gold in California, and now the war was drawing just the adventurous type of person the whale fishery so sorely needed.

By 1859, when the average age of the ships had reached almost 30 years, the Cold Spring fleet was beginning to show its years. As the industry waned, the vessels were sold off one by one. *Nathaniel P. Tallmadge* had already been returned to the packet service—out of New York—in 1855, while *Huntsville* was sold to New York interests in 1858. *Sheffield* and *Splendid* were both sold to Lang & Delano of Boston, probably ship brokers, in 1860. *Monmouth* set sail on her last voyage in August 1857. For almost five years she cruised the South Atlantic, South Pacific, Arctic and California grounds on one last "greasy" voyage.

Monmouth left Tahiti on February 9, 1862, and arrived at Valparaiso, Chile, on April 16, where she promptly placed her oil up for sale. While in port it was decided to end the voyage, so the ship was sold for $3,000 that May. The reasons are not known, but could well have been related to the ship's physical condition. *Monmouth* was 37 years old now and always had been rather leaky. Then, just about a year before she was sold, the old whaler, while going up Magdalena

Bay lagoon in Baja California, struck a sand bar. While she was aground her frame rose about 12 to 15 inches amidships, but when she slid off again, a short time later, resumed its proper place. Quite possibly this accident was a major factor contributing to her retirement.

Alice in October 1858 cleared for the Pacific, and was the last whaleship to sail from Cold Spring. This was a rather dull and uneventful 44-month voyage, during which she took only 90 barrels of sperm oil, about 1,600 barrels of whale oil and approximately 6,000 pounds of bone. Soon after *Alice* reached Cold Spring in June 1862 she was offered for sale, and Brown & Wilde of Boston purchased her for the merchant service on private terms that August. The following year she turned up at Liverpool, England, where she was sold again to foreign interests.

The demise of the whaling industry had short-ranging effects on the economy of the Cold Spring area, which had proven quite resilient in the past, and once again quickly recovered. Many of the former whalemen turned to the coasting trade or the oyster business, and soon after the Civil War some of them took to innkeeping, when the community became a popular summer resort for prosperous New Yorkers. As the years passed the whaling heritage of Cold Spring was slowly forgotten. But in 1932 a small number of public minded residents commissioned a plaque commemorating the village's earlier days as a whaling port. Placed prominently on the village green, it reads in part:

> From 1837 until the Petroleum Age began, The Village of Cold Spring Harbor, L. I. owned, manned, equipped & sailed a fleet of Whaling Vessels....
>
> In memory of these Ships, their daring Captains, hardy Sailors & foresighted Owners this testimonial is erected.

Then, in 1936, Dr. Robert Cushman Murphy, acting for the American Museum of Natural History, offered a fully equipped whaleboat to his friend, Dr. Charles B. Davenport, for display at Cold Spring Harbor. The boat had originally swung from the davits of the whaling brig *Daisy,* which had been built at Setauket, Long Island, in 1872. Dr. Murphy had sailed in *Daisy* out of New Bedford as Assistant Navigator for the 1912-1913 whaling season to the South Atlantic. With this nucleus, several leading citizens joined Dr. Davenport in incorporating the Whaling Museum Society that same year. And after a spirited campaign they were able to build a permanent home for the boat by 1942, when the doors of the Cold Spring Harbor Whaling

Museum opened for its first season. Today, the museum has expanded from one small room containing Dr. Davenport's own sizeable collection of relics to four rooms chocked to the gunwales with every sort of whaling item, including many curios culled from local cellars and attics.

The little village has changed greatly over the past century. While the whaleships are long gone, it is still possible to take a stroll through Cold Spring today and to picture—in the mind's eye—knots of swarthy men, speaking loudly in strange tongues, making their way down Bedlam Street in search of an inviting place in which to spend their lays. Several of the old whalers' houses and familiar places still stand on that Main Street. Manuel Enos' home lies across from the Whaling Museum and that of DeWitt Barrett is still just a few doors away.

Just to the west outside the village proper the road takes a slight bend. The whaling company wharf which stood nearby is gone now, but if you are brave enough to tramp down through the brush, the foundations of the old Jones Mill can still be found. The Jones Store, which was the "home office" for the whalers, is long gone, having been destroyed by fire many years ago. But it is not too difficult to stand there and imagine John H. Jones, working by an oil lamp at a huge cubbyhole desk, penning a letter to one of his far-off captains, or perhaps, standing at the store counter issuing a first whaling outfit to a greenhand.

Turn right at the modern intersection and you chance on old St. John's Church, where the Joneses and some of the whalemen used to worship. Alongside the church is a stately marble monument honoring the achievements of that favorite village son, Walter Restored Jones. Cross the highway, on grounds presently maintained by the Long Island Biological Association and the Carnegie Institution of Washington, and you will find the last vestiges of Bungtown. The storehouses, cooper shops and lofts of the whaling days are gone now, save for one or two small warehouse buildings, but some of the original stately homes, dating to the whaling era, still exist.

We break our reverie and suddenly realize that the whaling days are gone forever, but the ships and men that sailed from this tiny port of Cold Spring are not forgotten so easily. They have left their mark, however small, in maritime history from home at Cold Spring Harbor to the fringes of the Antarctic, the Atlantic, Pacific and Indian Oceans, as well as the mysterious and treacherous waters of the Arctic. And so passed an industry which helped make America great . . . .

Glossary

baleen whale	Whales having long fibrous bone (baleen) in mouth to strain food from sea water
barrel	On whaleship; unit of measure (31½ gallons)
blubber	Fatty tissue of whale
blubber hook	Used with cutting tackle to strip blubber from whale
boatsteerer	Harpooner; steered while mate attempted to kill whale
break out	Take out of storage
bung	Stopper in cask or barrel
caboose	Small deckhouse or galley
capstan	Revolving vertical drum for lifting anchor or heavy loads
clew	Haul sails up to yard or mast
cooper	Ship's barrel maker
cutting in	Process of stripping blubber from a whale
cutting stage	Platform suspended over ship's side from which officers cut in with spades
cutting tackle	Block-and-tackle used with blubber hook to hoist pieces of blubber aboard ship
drogue	Keg or block of wood to check speed of whale just as line was about to run out
fluke chains	Used to secure a dead whale to side of ship
flukes	Horizontal tail fins of a whale
fo'c's'le	Also, "forecastle." Deck and crew spaces in bow

GLOSSARY

greasy	Whalers' term for "good," "successful"
gurry	Slimy residue from the cutting in
halliards	Ropes for hoisting sails, flags, etc.
Kanaka	Pacific Island native
krill	Shrimp-like, crustacean food of baleen whale
lance	Long-handled instrument used to kill whale
lay	Whaleman's share in earnings of voyage
marlinspike	Tapered, pointed iron spike for splicing rope
masthead rings	Lookout stood in when scanning for whales
Nantucket sleigh ride	A boat fast to a wild, fleeing whale
outfits	Equipment for a whaling voyage
packet	Ship sailing on a regular schedule
recruits	Fresh food and supplies
shooks	Barrel staves
shrouds	Lines supporting masts
slops	Clothing, personal items sold to sailors during voyage
spade	Long-handled, flat, broadbladed instrument to cut in
spunyarn	Twine made from the strands of old rope; for baling stacks of whalebone
toothed whale	As distinguished from baleen whale; have teeth to seize and grasp prey
try out	To render oil from blubber
trypot	Huge 200-gallon cauldrons set in tryworks
tryworks	Brick ovens set on deck; supported trypots
whalebone	Same as baleen
whalecraft	Tools of the trade, included harpoons, lances, spades, etc.

Selected Bibliography

MANUSCRIPTS

(A) Collections

Atlantic Mutual Insurance Company, New York: Disaster books, policy records.

John D. Hewlett, Wilmington, Del.: Phoebe E. H. Willets Collection.

Melville Whaling Room, New Bedford (Mass.) Free Public Library: Dennis Wood "Abstracts."

National Archives, Washington, D. C.: Record groups 21, 41, 59, 78 and 267.

Public Archives, Port Louis, Mauritius: Volume RA 1224.

Public Record Office, London, England: CO 167/363 and ADM 7/189.

Whaling Museum Society, Inc., Cold Spring Harbor, N. Y.: Jones, Stoddard and Taylor Collections.

(B) Diaries, Memoirs and Treatises

Rogers, Helen. Diary, 1843-1850. Whaling Museum Society, Inc.

Roys, Thomas Welcome. "Description of Whales," written aboard whaleship *Sheffield*, 1854, Mariners Museum, Newport News, Virginia.

———. "Voyages of Capt. Thomas Welcome Roys," Suffolk County Whaling Museum, Sag Harbor, N. Y.

(C) Logs and Journals

Alice, 1854-1858. Whaling Museum Society, Inc.

Alice, 1858-1860. Chester Abrams, Jr., Walla Walla, Wash.
Edgar, 1852-1855. (Microfilm). Whaling and Marine Manuscript Archives, Nantucket, Mass.
Monmouth, 1843-1845. East Hampton (N. Y.) Free Library.
Nathaniel P. Tallmadge, 1843-1845, 1848-1851. East Hampton Free Library.
Richmond, 1843-1844. Queens Borough Public Library, Jamaica, N. Y.
Sheffield, 1845-1849 (Printed copy). Historical Collection, Town of Brookhaven, Patchogue, N. Y.
Sheffield, 1849-1850, Marine Historical Association, Mystic, Conn.
Splendid, 1848-1851 (Microfilm). Whaling and Marine Manuscript Archives.
Tuscarora, 1839-1841. East Hampton Free Library.

PRINTED DOCUMENTS

British Patent Office. No. 965 dated April 16, 1859 and No. 450 dated February 22, 1861.
Jones et al v. *The Richmond,* District Court, Southern District, New York, 1853, 13 *Federal Cases* 1008-1012, Case no. 7,491.
Jones v. *The Richmond,* District Court, Southern District, New York, 1858, 13 *Federal Cases* 1012-1013, Case no. 7,492.
New York (State) Legislature, Assembly, *Journal,* 61st Session. Albany: Croswell, 1838.
New York (State) Legislature, Senate, *Journal,* 61st Session. Albany: Croswell, 1838.
———. *Session Laws, 1838,* CH. 106, "An Act to incorporate the Cold Spring Whaling Company." Passed, March 24, 1838.
———. *Session Laws, 1840,* CH. 182, "An Act to revive and amend the act to incorporate the Cold Spring Whaling Company." Passed, April 28, 1840.
Post et al. v. *Jones et al.* The Supreme Court of the United States, 1856, 19 *Howard* (60 *United States Reports*) 150-162.
Supreme Court of the United States no. 132. *Wm. K. Post and Al., Claimants of the Cargo, &C., of the Ship Richmond, Appt's* v. *John H. Jones and Al., Libellants.* Appeal from

the Circuit Court U.S. for the Southern District of New York.
U.S. Supreme Court Records, 19 *Howard* (1855).

U.S. Patent Office. No. 31,190 dated January 22, 1861; No. 35,474 dated June 3, 1862; No. 35,475 dated June 3, 1862; No. 35,977 dated July 22, 1862; No. 54,211 dated April 24, 1866 and No. 214,707 dated April 22, 1879.

NEWSPAPERS AND JOURNALS

British Colonist (Victoria, B.C., Canada) 1868-1871.
Commercial Gazette (Port Louis, Mauritius) September 28, October 5 and 8, 1853.
Corrector (Sag Harbor, N.Y.) 1836-1862.
Daily Advertiser (Boston, Mass.) May 27, 1848; May 13 and 15, 1851.
Eagle (Brooklyn, N.Y.) September 13, 1903.
Empire (Sydney, N.S.W., Australia) November 18, 1853; August 16, 1854.
Evening Journal (Albany, N.Y.) February 2, 1838.
Express (Sag Harbor, N.Y.) 1860-1862.
Friend, The (Honolulu, Hawaii) November 1, 1848; October 1, 1849; and September 1855.
Illustrated London News December 10, 1853.
Inquirer (Hempstead, N.Y.) June 22 and 29, 1836.
Long Islander (Huntington, N.Y.) 1839-1862; March 16, 1895.
Morning Chronicle (London, England) December 2, 1853.
New York Times April 20, 1890; November 12, 1932.
Nordanfari (Akureyri, Iceland) Various issues 1863-1868.
Pjódólfr (Reykjavik, Iceland) 1865-1866.
Post (Boston, Mass.) May 13, 1851.
Shipping Gazette and Sydney General Trade List (Sydney, N.S.W., Australia) January 25, February 1, March 1 and 29, November 29 and December 6, 1851.
Whalemen's Shipping List and Merchant's Transcript (New Bedford, Mass.) 1843-1862; March 5, 1867.

ARTICLES

Bailey, Paul. "Fast Deal In Whaleoil," *Long Islander,* (Huntington, N.Y.), March 30, 1961.
Bleecker, T. Bache. "Cold Spring Harbor Whaling," Long Island *Forum,* October 1943.
Dumont, Peter L. "Adventures of an American Whaleman,"

Frank Leslie's Illustrated Newspaper, March 26, 1859.

Horton, H. P. "Jonas Winters, Whaling Captain," Long Island *Forum,* August 1948.

Johnsen, Arne Odd. "The Shell Harpoon," *Norsk Hvalfangst-Tidende* (The Norwegian *Whaling Gazette*), September 1940.

Norman, Carl. *"Hval-, hvalros-og saelhundefangstens historie og udvikling." Tidsskrift for Søvaesen,* (Copenhagen), 1866-1867.

S(leight), H.(arry) D. "Gone for 24 Years, Whaling Bark *Andrew Hicks* Returns," *Leader,* (Babylon, N.Y.), April 15, 1927.

———. "Pen Pictures of Ye Olden East End Whaling Skippers," *Leader,* May 6, 1927.

Smith, Sandra Truxtun. "The Whaling Industry in Poughkeepsie (1830-1845)." *Yearbook,* (Dutchess County Historical Society, Poughkeepsie, N.Y.), 1956.

Tooker, James E. "Whalers Stage Rescue," Long Island *Forum,* November 1943.

Tvede, ———. *"Den amerikanske hvalfanger-virksomhed under Island i 1865-66," Tidsskrift for Fiskeri,* (Copenhagen), 1867.

Valentine, Andrus. " 'Big Manuel,' Whaling Captain," Long Island *Forum,* March 1954.

Wilford, Sarah, "Cold Spring Harbor Was Busy Whaling Town," Long Island *Press,* January 11, 1936.

Books and Pamphlets

Adams, James Truslow. *Memorials of Old Bridgehampton.* Bridgehampton, N.Y.: Privately published, 1916.

Albion, Robert Greenhalgh. *The Rise of New York Port* (1815-1860). Hamden, Conn.: Archon Books, 1961.

———. *Square-Riggers on Schedule.* Hamden, Conn.: Archon Books, 1965.

Ashley, Clifford W. *The Yankee Whaler.* (Second ed.) Garden City, N.Y.: Halcyon House, 1942.

Bailey, Paul. *Long Island Whalers.* Amityville, N.Y.: Paul Bailey, 1959.

Bayles, Richard M. *Historical and Descriptive Sketches of Suffolk County.* Port Jefferson, N.Y.: 1874.

Cold Spring Harbor Library. Cold Spring Harbor, N.Y.: (n.p.), 1914.

Cold Spring Harbor Soundings. Cold Spring Harbor: Village Improvement Society, 1953.

Cosgrove, J. N. *Gray Days and Gold.* New York: The Atlantic Companies, 1967.

Cutler, Carl C. *Five Hundred Sailing Records of American Built Ships.* Mystic, Conn.: Marine Historical Association, 1952.

——. *Greyhounds of the Sea.* Annapolis, Md.: U.S. Naval Institute, 1961.

——. *Queens of the Western Ocean.* Annapolis: U. S. Naval Institute, 1961.

Dakin, William J. *Whalemen Adventurers.* (Rev. ed.) Sydney, N.S.W., Aust.: Angus & Robertson, 1963.

Duvall, Ralph G. *The History of Shelter Island.* Shelter Island Heights, N.Y.: Privately printed, 1932.

Earle, Walter K. *Concerning the Whaling Museum at Cold Spring Harbor. . . .* Cold Spring Harbor. Whaling Museum Society, 1961.

——. *Out of the Wilderness.* Cold Spring Harbor: Whaling Museum Society, 1966.

——. *Scrimshaw, Folk Art of the Whalers.* Cold Spring Harbor: Whaling Museum Society, 1957.

——. *The Ships "Richmond" and "Edgar", of Cold Spring.* Cold Spring Harbor: Whaling Museum Society, 1948.

——. *Sketches of Yankee Whaling.* No. 1, "Something About Whales;" No. 2, "How They Captured the Whales;" No. 3, "How They 'Processed' the Whales." Cold Spring Harbor: Whaling Museum Society, (n.d.).

Fairburn, William A. *Merchant Sail.* (6 vols.) Center Lovell, Me.: Fairburn Marine Educational Foundation, 1945-1955.

Foote, Don C. "Exploration and Resource Utilization in Northwestern Arctic Alaska before 1855." Ph.D. diss. Montreal: McGill University, 1965.

Hohman, Elmo P. *The American Whaleman.* New York: Longmans, Green, 1928.

Howell, Nathaniel R. *Long Island Whaling.* Bay Shore, N.Y.: Long Island *Forum,* 1941.

SELECTED BIBLIOGRAPHY

Johnsen, Arne Odd. *Den Moderne Hvalfangsts Historie.* (Vol. I) Oslo, Norway: H. Aschehoug & Co., 1959.

Jones, John H. *The Jones Family of Long Island.* New York: Tobias A. Wright, 1907.

Laing, Alexander. *Clipper Ships and Their Makers.* New York: G. P. Putnam's Sons, 1966.

Laughlin, Harry, H. "Broken Harpoon from the 'Bark Alice.'" Cold Spring Harbor: (Mimeo. flyer), 1931.

Lubbock, Basil. *The Western Ocean Packets.* Boston: Charles E. Lauriat, 1925.

Lutwyche, Alfred J. P. *A Narrative of the Wreck of the Meridian on the Island of Amsterdam.* Sydney, N.S.W., Aust.: Waugh and Cox, 1854.

Murphy, Robert Cushman. *The Founding of the Whaling Museum At Cold Spring Harbor, L.I., N.Y.* Cold Spring Harbor: Whaling Museum Society, 1967.

Norris, Martin J. *The Law of Salvage.* Mount Kisco, N.Y.: Baker, Voohris, 1958.

———.*Law of Seaman.* (2 Vols.) New York: Baker, Voohris, 1951.

Overton, Jacqueline. *Long Island's Story.* Garden City, N.Y.: Doubleday, Doran, 1929.

Palmer, W. R. "The Whaling Port of Sag Harbor." Ph.D. diss. New York: Columbia University, 1959.

Sammis, Romanah. *Huntington-Babylon Town History.* Huntington, N.Y.: Huntington Historical Society, 1937.

Scammon, Charles M. *The Marine Mammals of the Northwestern Coast of North America. . . .* San Francisco: J. H. Carmany, 1874.

Sleight, Harry D. *The Whale Fishery on Long Island.* Bridgehampton, N.Y.: Hampton Press, 1931.

Starbuck, Alexander. *History of the American Whale Fishery.* Washington: Government Printing Office, 1878.

Thompson, Benjamin F. *History of Long Island.* New York: E. French, 1839.

Townsend, Charles H. *The Distribution of Certain Whales as Shown by Logbook Records of American Whaleships.* (*Zoologica,* Vol. XIX, No. 1) New York Zoological Society, 1935.

Twelve Hours on the Wreck; or, The Stranding of the Sheffield. New York: T. C. Butler, 1844.

Valentine, H. G. and A. T., and Newman, E. V. *Main Street, Cold Spring Harbor.* Huntington, N.Y.: Huntington Historical Society, 1960.

Watson, Arthur C. *The Long Harpoon.* New Bedford, Mass.: Reynolds Printing, 1929.

Whaling Museum Society. *Annual Reports,* 1943-1970.

Appendices

APPENDIX I COLD SPRING HARBOR WHALING VOYAGES

Year Ship	Captain	Whaling Grounds	Sailed Date/Port	Arrived	Duration
1836 *Monmouth*	Richard S. Topping	SA	7/18SH	4/10/37	8½ mos.
1837 *Monmouth*	David Smith	SA	7/-	5/8/38	10 mos.
Tuscarora	William Dennison	SA-IO	9/9	4/23/39	19½ mos.
1838 *Monmouth*	Smith	SA	7/17NY	5/24/39NY	10 mos.
1839 *Monmouth*	Charles Bennett	SA	7/27NY	5/3/40SH	9 mos.
Tuscarora	Edward Halsey	SA-IO-SP	7/27	5/25/41	22 mos.
1840 *Monmouth*	William H. Hedges	SA-IO	8/4SH	6/19/41	10½ mos.
1841 *Monmouth*	William H. Hedges	SA-IO	9/25	6/25/42	9 mos.
Tuscarora	Eli H. White	SA-IO-SP	8/3	6/26/43	22½ mos.
1842 *Monmouth*	Hiram B. Hedges	SA-IO	8/13	7/11/43	11 mos.
1843 *Monmouth*	Hiram B. Hedges	SA-CH-SP	10/11	1/1/46	26½ mos.
1844 *N. P. Tallmadge*	William H. Hedges	NWC-CAL SA-SP-NWC-IO	6/14NY	2/19/45NY	20 mos.
Richmond	Jeremiah Ludlam	NWC-SP	12/2	3/13/46	27 mos.
Tuscarora	Eli H. White	NWC-OK-SP	9/23	5/26/45	20 mos.
1845 *Alice*	Freeman H. Smith	NWC-SP	9/18	6/17/46	21 mos.
Huntsville	George T. Howe	NWC-SP	10/23	6/29/47	32 mos.
Splendid	Henry C. Fordham	NWC-SP	6/28	4/26/48	46 mos.
1846 *N. P. Tallmadge*	Jeremiah Mulford	SA-NWC-SP	6/5	5/1/48	35 mos.
Sheffield	Eli H. White	SA-NWC-OK	11/11	2/7/49NY	39 mos.
Tuscarora	Elisha Doane	CH-SP	8/12	3/24/48	31½ mos.
1846 *Alice*	John Woolley	NWC-CAL	9/3	4/27/49	31½ mos.
Monmouth	Edward Halsey	SA-SP-CH-IO	3/13NY	8/8/50NY	53 mos.
Richmond	Philander R. Winters	SA-IO-NWC BS-OK-SP	7/21	Wrecked in Bering Strait, 8/2/49	
1847 *Huntsville*	Freeman H. Smith	SP-OK	9/30	4/21/49	18½ mos.
1848 *N. P. Tallmadge*	Jeremiah Mulford	SP-NWC	9/26	3/26/51	30 mos.
Splendid	Samuel B. Pierson	SP-NWC-OK	10/28	3/15/51	28½ mos.
Tuscarora	Samuel C. Leek	SP-IO-BS	8/3	Sold, Sydney, 3/51	

138

APPENDICES

Year Ship	Captain	Whaling Grounds	Sailed Date/Port	Arrived	Duration
1849					
Alice	Richard P. Smith	SP-BS	8/17	3/23/51	19 mos.
Huntsville	Freeman H. Smith	SP-BS	10/26	3/21/51	17 mos.
Sheffield	Thomas W. Roys	SP-OK-BS	8/17 NY	1/23/54 NY	53 mos.
1851					
Alice	Eli H. White	SP-BS	10/6	4/13/54	30 mos.
Huntsville	Freeman H. Smith	SP-OK	12/4	4/7/54	28 mos.
Monmouth	Isaac Ludlow	SA-IO	8/28	5/3/54	31 mos.
N. P. Tallmadge	Henry H. Edwards	SP-NWC-A	10/3	4/26/55	43 mos.
Splendid	Richard P. Smith	SP-OK-BS	10/15	4/12/53	18 mos.
1852					
Edgar	Samuel B. Pierson	SP-OK	11/25	Wrecked in Okhotsk Sea, 6/5/55	
1853					
Splendid	Richard P. Smith	OK	11/30	4/4/56	28 mos.
1854					
Alice	George G. Penney	SP-OK	10/31	4/24/58	42 mos.
Huntsville	William James Grant	SP-OK-NWC	10/15	5/6/58	42½ mos.
Monmouth	Jerimiah Eldredge	SA-SP-IO	11/28	6/2/57	30 mos.
Sheffield	H. J. Green	SP-OK-CAL	9/12	5/4/59	56 mos.
1856					
Splendid	Samuel B. Pierson	SP-OK-CAL	9/15	4/27/60	43½ mos.
1857					
Monmouth	Hiram B. Ormesby	SA-SP-OK-CAL	8/22	Sold, Valparaiso, 5/62	
1858					
Alice	William S. Beebe	SP-OK-CAL	10/—	6/8/62	44 mos.

1. ABBREVIATION KEY: A=Arctic Ocean; BS=Bering Strait; CAL=California; CH=Chile; SH=Sag Harbor; IO=Indian Ocean; NWC=North West Coast (Alaska); NY=New York City; OK=Sea of Okhotsk; SA=South Atlantic; SP=South Pacific.

2. NOTES:
  A. This table is adapted from Alexander Starbuck's *History of the American Whale Fishery* with corrections and additions.
  B. Starbuck lists a voyage for the bark *Barclay* for 1839. From examination of customs records and contemporary newspapers, it has been established that this was a printer's error, as the voyage actually was made from Westport, Mass.
  C. Every effort was made to include a table of "takings" of oil and whalebone for each voyage. While the amounts actually landed at the end of each voyage are listed in Starbuck, these statistics are misleading in that they do not reflect—in many cases—oil and bone which was sold overseas to cover expenses, as well as consignments shipped to better markets or back to the U. S. Unfortunately all attempts at researching and producing such a table were met with partial, conflicting and incomplete information. In the interests of accuracy these tables have been omitted.

APPENDIX II

AN ACT *to incorporate the Cold Spring Whaling Company.*
Passed March 24, 1838.

The People of the State of New-York, represented in Senate and Assembly, do enact as follows:

1. William Jones, John H. Jones, Richard M. Conklin, Abner Chichester, Zophar B. Oakley, Henry Willis, Samuel J. Underhill, Daniel Rogers and Walter R. Jones, and such others as now are or hereafter may be associated with them, for the purpose of engaging in the whale fisheries in the Atlantic and Pacific oceans and elsewhere, and in the manufacture of oil and spermaceti candles, and in erecting dock accommodations in Cold Spring harbor, are hereby constituted a body corporate by the name of "The Cold Spring Whaling Company," to be located in the village of Cold Spring, in the town of Oyster Bay, Queens county.

2. The subscription book to the capital stock shall be opened under the direction of William Jones, John H. Jones, Richard M. Conklin, John Willis and Samuel Underhill, or a majority of them, who are hereby appointed commissioners for that purpose, and are authorized to receive subscriptions to the said capital stock, at such time and place in Cold Spring as they shall appoint; and five dollars on each share subscribed, shall be paid to the said commissioners at the time of subscribing, to be subsequently handed over to the company after its organization; and the stock shall be distributed as the commissioners may deem most advantageous to the interests of said corporation.

3. The capital stock of the said corporation shall be one hundred thousand dollars, and be divided into shares of fifty dollars each: but it shall be lawful for the said corporation when the whole capital

shall have been subscribed, and fifty thousand dollars of the said capital stock shall have been paid in, to commence business, and with that capital to conduct and carry on the same, until they shall deem it expedient to call in their remaining capital: and the said corporation is further authorized to collect subscriptions at such time and in such amounts as they may deem proper, and to receive in payment vessels or shares in vessels or other property, at such valuations as may be affixed thereto by the commissioners, or by the board of directors; and the corporation shall also have power to forfeit the shares of subscribers on the non-payment of any instalment, and also to declare dividends on the stock.

4. The stock, property, affairs and concerns of the said corporation shall be managed by nine directors, who shall choose one out of their number to be president and another to be vice-president, all of whom shall hold their offices till the first Monday in December of each year, and until others are chosen: the first election of directors shall be under the inspection of the commissioners before named, or a majority of them: and subsequent elections shall be held under the inspection of three stockholders, not directors, to be chosen by the board of directors; and notice of the election of directors shall be given ten days prior to its taking place, in one of the newspapers in the county: and at such election each stockholder shall be entitled to one vote for each share held: and if any vacancy shall happen during a year, the board shall have power to fill the same for the remainder of the term.

5. The stock shall be deemed personal property, and no transfer shall be deemed valid, unless made on the books to be kept by the company.

6. The corporation shall be authorized to purchase and hold real estate to an amount not exceeding twenty-five thousand dollars.

7. The corporation shall be continued for twenty years and shall possess the power and be subject to the provisions of the eighteenth chapter of the first part of the Revised Statutes, so far as the same are applicable.

8. The legislature may alter, repeal or modify this act.

9. No foreigner shall ever be a stockholder, or in any way interested in said company.

APPENDIX III

List of Persons Comprising the Crew of the *Ship Tuscarora* of *Cold Spring* whereof is Master *Eli H. White* bound for *the South Seas* on *a Whaling Voyage*

Names	Places of Birth	Places of Residence	of What Country Citizens or Subjects	Aged	Height ft ins	Complexion	Hair
Eli H. White	So. Hampton	So. Hampton	United States	28	5 10½	light	brown
Wm F. Fowler	do	do	do	27	6	fair	do
Albert Halsey	do	do	do	24	5 8	do	dark
Ths Warren	New York	do	do	25	5 6½	do	do
Geo. Dugand	London	do	do	23	5 8½	do	brown
Wm Sayer	So. Hampton	do	do	20	5 5	fair	Sandy
Treadwell Rowland	Commack	Huntington	do	21	5 6	do	do
Robt Reen	Calais	Cold Spring	do	24	5 5½	do	dark
John Egan	New York	New York	do	27	5 6½	do	do
John Flint	Edinburg	Cold Spring	do	30	5 5	Mulatto	Curley
Jason Jack	E. Hampton	do	do	22	5 5½	Blk	Woolly
Wm Shanks	Oyster Bay	do	do	21	5 11½	Florid	Brown
Uriah Hendrickson	do	do	do	22	5 9	light	dark
Edward M. Jones	Cold Spring	do	do	21	5 9¾	dark	dark
Zebulon Rodgers	do	do	do	22	5 9¾	do	brown
Henry Titus	do	do	do	19	5 11	light	brown
Chas. M. Halsted	Pittstown	Troy	do	20	5 7	Sallow	dark
Alfred Gall	Oyster Bay	Cold Spring	do	20	5 6	Coloured	Curley
Roderick Ryin	Islip	do	do	22	5 9	do	do
Antone F. DeFragra	Fayall	do	do	21	5 9	dark	dark
Waterman Reed	New Zealand	do	New Zealand	23	5 10	Yellow	Black
James Canack	Society Island	do	Society Islands	24	5 8	do	do
John Canack	do	do	do	23	5 7	do	do
Thos Canack	So. Hampton	do	do	25	5 10	do	do
Saml Halsey	So. Hampton	So. Hampton	do	16	5 9	fair	dark

(Signed)

Addison J. Rher	do	do	U. States	21	5 10	Colr	brown Woolly
John Fowler	do	do		14	5 2	fair	dark

Eli H. White

Elias Van Cott	Cold Spring	Cold Spring	United States	24	5 5½	Light	Brown
Jackson Valentine	Oyster Bay, L.I.	Oyster Bay	United States	34	5 10½	Light	Black
George Jerome	New York City	Cold Spring	United States	19	5 6½	Mullatto	Woolly
Henry Payne	Oyster bay LI	Oyster bay LI.	United States	20	5 5	Black	Woolly
Edward Foster	Southampton LI	Southampton	United States	22	5 4¾	fair	Brown

From the Jones Collection, Cold Spring Harbor Whaling Museum

APPENDIX IV

"List of things on board Bk *Monmouth,* Augt 16, 1851"

30 Spade poles	4½ Manilla 2 coils	4 Casks old Flour
5 Large spruce poles	5½ inch Do I	4 Casks Old Tow lines
8 Bundles codfish	2½ Do 2	Cutting blocks
700 lbs Hams	3 inch M 3	1 Coil Old Towline
3 Barels Beans	2-¾ M 4	5 Stearing oars
2 Barels Mackerel	2 inch 3	12 sixteen foot oars
2 Barels Sugar	Spunyarn 4	24 Do 18 foot oars
1 Box Sugar	Marline 1	1 Cooler
1 Cask Rice	15 thread Ratline 1	1 Deck pot
3 Barels Corn Meal	Lance wash 1	Lat Potatoes
8 bags Butter	Bone yard 2	1 Box Old Tobacco
3 Bags Coffee	hamberlines 1	20 Barels Sand
4 Boxes Tobacco	1-½ inch Manilla 2	200 Barrels Provision
3 Boxes mustard	Hemp Towlines 2 coils	Beef and Pork
2 Boxes soap	Manilla towlis 14	1 bask Flags
11 Casks Molasses	1 Spare try pot	23 Plank
2 Tons Hoops	2 fin chains	133 Boards
1 Roll Leather	1 hand lead line and head	
3 Boxes Tea	1 Lagline	
9 Cheeses	1 Deep sea line and lead	
13 basks Bread	2 coils Old bone yarn	
7 Barels Vinegar	½ bil old——fall	
2 Boxes Rivets	6 coils hemp rigging from loft	
2 Grind Stones	½ coil Houslin	
300 feet Heading	2 Boat Compasses	
300 feet Boat boards	4 Marine Compasses	
100 staves	1 Coper pump	
4 Casks Old Bread	bat Boat nees and timbers	
5 basks sails		
1 Cask Old Meat		

FROM the Jones Collection, Cold Spring Harbor Whaling Museum.

APPENDIX V

"Ship Splendid" Cap. R. P. Smith
Slops Sold to the Crew

[undated, but probably c. 1851-1853]

old wool hats	shaving brushes	soap
suspenders	striped shirts	needles
tobacco	blue dungarees	reefing jackets
thin boots	buttons	scotch caps
sheath & belts	oil coats	guernsey frocks
knives	oil pants	south westers
pumps	thick shoes	drawers
blue dungaree pieces	old pumps	coats
brown cloth	socks	razor strap
white cloth	tarpaulin hats	comforters
pipes	woolen pants	old flannel shirts
calico	flannel shirts	slippers
chests	thick boots	lamps
blankets	duck pants	palms
pepper sauce	forks	beds
wicks	spoons	boots
deep pans	pocket knives	flannel under shirts
tin pots	combs	
razors	thread	
shaving boxes		

FROM the Jones Collection, Cold Spring Harbor Whaling Museum.

APPENDIX VI

WHALESHIP MEDICINE CHEST

(This is a typical Cold Spring Harbor medicine chest reconstructed from old pharmacists' bills)

ITEM:	USED FOR:
Adhesive plaster	Covering wounds, abrasions, etc.
Blue Vitriol (Sulphate of Copper)	Astringent, tonic, also for intermittent fevers, epilepsy, other spasmatic diseases, croup, chronic diarrhea, discharging poisons.
Castor oil	Cathartic.
Ceratum Resinae	Balm for treating blisters, sores, burns and scalds.
Elixir of Vitriol (Aromatic Sulphuric Acid)	Tonic, astringent, also helpful in relieving fevers and scurvy.
Enema syringe	Used in administering purging medicines.
Epsom salt (Sulphate of Magnesia)	Cathartic.
Essence of Peppermint	Relieving colic, indigestion.
Flax seed	Very soothing; used for respiratory complaints, dysentary, kidney and bladder stones, and other urinary and intestinal inflamations.
Injection, purging powders	Enemas.
Lancets	Minor surgery.
Laudanum (Tincture of opium)	Relieving pain, sedative.
Liquor Plumbi Subacetatis (Solution of Subacetate of Lead)	Astringent and sedative for sprains, bruises, burns and blisters.
Medical book	There were numerous books of directions for laymen, published both in the U.S. and abroad during the 19th century, with some prepared especially for shipboard use.
Paregoric elixir (Camphorated tincture of Opium)	Tuberculosis, coughs, asthma, nausea, diarrhea and stomach and bowel cramps.
Peruvian bark (Quinine)	Relieving fevers.
Stick caustic	Probably silver nitrate molded into stick form for use as a caustic pencil.
Sulphur	Laxative, inducing sweating; also helpful in treating rheumatism, gout and respiratory illnesses.
Sweet Oil (Olive oil)	Mild laxative; protection for skin
Tooth claw	Dental extractions.
Turlington's Balsam of Life (a compound Benzoin Tincture)	A widely used patent medicine; astringent, antiseptic.

From the Jones Collection, Cold Spring Harbor Whaling Museum

Index

Abbot, Scudder, 44-45, 58
Absecon Beach, N. J., 22
Admiralty Court, 111
Aitutaki, Cook Is., 60-61
Alaska, 99, 104, 118
Albion, Robert G., 7
Aleutian Is., Alaska, 37, 103
Allen, Capt. Francis P., 21
Allyn, Capt. William, 61
American Museum of Natural History, 126
Amsterdam Is., Ind. O., 71-82
Anadir, Gulf of, U.S.S.R., 86
Antarctica, 107, 127
Arctic Ocean, 34, 38, 39, 56, 63, 86, 94, 95, 100, 102, 103-106, 123, 124, 125
Ascension Is., Pac., 66
Atlantic City, N. J., 22
Atlantic Insurance Co., 7
Atlantic Mutual Insurance Co., 7, 18
Atlantic Ocean, 21, 32, 63, 69, 127
Australia, 13, 33, 41, 70
Azores Is., 13, 26, 34, 35, 99

Babcock, Charles, 52, 54
Baffin Is., Can., 108
Baja California, Mex., 33, 126
Baltimore, Md., 13, 17
Baltimore clippers, 17
Barclay Sound, B.C., Can., 116
Barnes, Capt. Thomas D., 66
Barnet, James F., 57
Barrett, DeWitt, 42, 98, 99, 127
Barrett, Freeman, 98

Barrett, George W., 42, 98, 99
"Bedlam Street," 120, 127
Beebe, Capt. William S., 68
Bering Strait, 17, 33-34, 84, 86, 98, 102, 103-104
Bermuda, 40, 52
Betts, Hon. Samuel R., 94
Billings, N. & W. W., 10, 14
Biscay, Bay of, 109
Bishop, Rogers, 110
Black Ball Line, 20, 21
Blackmer, Capt. Seth M., 95-96
Blair, James, 67
Blue Swallowtail Line, 21
Bomb lance, 50, 109
Boston, Mass., 8, 14, 125, 126
Bowen's bomb gun, 108
Brand, C. C., 50, 109
Bridgehampton, L. I., 8, 83, 94
British Columbia, Can., 115-117
Brooklyn, N. Y., 8, 83
Brower, William, 79
Brown, Benjamin's Sons, 107-109
Brown, John B., 21
Brown & Wilde, 126
Brunswick, Me., 21
Brush, Susan, 99
Bucksport, Me., 4
"Bungtown," 24, 119, 127
Burton, Robert, 14

Calhoun, Capt. Rufus, 116
California, 29, 33, 60, 118, 125; gold rush, 29, 33, 60, 105, 124, 125
Canada, 26, 102, 115

"Cannon Hill," 119
Canton, China, 17
Cape Town, South Africa, 55, 63
Carnegie Institution, 127
Carr, John P., 90
Chanties, 54
Charlestown, Mass., 14
Cherry, William, 91
Cheyney, Capt. J. H., 14
Chichester, Abner, 10
Chile, 26
Chilean grounds, 34
China clippers, 13, 17
Chukchi Pen., U.S.S.R., 87
Church, Capt. C. S., 50
Civil War, 125, 126
Cochran, Capt. David, 68-69
Cold Spring (Harbor), L. I., 4-5, 6, 7, 8, 10, 11, 12, 14, 15, 16, 17, 20, 21, 22, 23, 24, 25, 26, 29, 33, 35, 39, 42, 45, 81, 85, 91, 95, 96, 97, 98, 99, 100, 101, 106, 119, 120, 123, 124, 125, 126, 127
Cold Spring Harbor Whaling Museum, 46, 126-127
Cold Spring Steam Boat Co., 6
Cold Spring Whaling Co., 10-12
Collins, Edward K., 19
Confederate States, 125
Congreve, Sir William, 113-114
Congreve rocket, 110, 113-114
Conklin, Richard M., 10
Cook, Capt. James, R.N., 13
Cook's Straits, N. Z., 16
Cope, Henry and Thomas P., 14
Cope Line, 14
Corlear's Hook, N. Y. C., 20
Corrector, Sag Harbor, L. I., 9
Cousteau, Jacques, 3
Crews: deserters, 35; integration, 26; mutinies, 58-63, 69, 105; nationalities, 26; outfitting, 29-30; pay (lays), 26-28, 35, 121, 122-123; rates and duties, 27-28; recruitment, 25, 29, 35; sickness, 36, 55-58; typical, 25-26
Crozet Is., 33, 99, 103
Cuffee, Nathaniel P., 94
Culver, John, 57
Cumberland Inlet, Can., 108

Dalton, John, 59
Danish Fishery Co., 114
Darwin, Charles, 34

Davenport, Dr. Charles B., 126-127
Davis Strait, Green., 108
Deep Bay, B. C., Can., 116
Dehan, Henry, 78
Dennison, Capt. William, 10
Dimon, John, 20
Documents, whaling, 9, 9n.
Douglass, Capt., 53
Dugan, William T., 17
Dumont, Peter, 31, 41-42, 64
Dundee, Scotland, 113
Dutchess Whaling Co., 16
Duval, William R., 43

Eagle Line, 17, 22
Earl, Capt. William, 96
Earle, Walter K., 46
East Hampton, L. I., 8, 100
East River, N. Y. C., 20
Edenton, N. C., 4
Edwards, Capt. Henry, 24
Eldredge, Capt. Jerimiah, 31, 41-44, 62-63, 83
Eldridge, Capt. John, 19-20
England, 26, 110, 111
Enos, Ella Nora, 100
Enos, Capt. Manuel, 41, 99-100, 127
Enos, Melna, 99, 100
Eskimos, 39, 45, 87-88
Europe, 108
Excelsior Fireworks Co., 112

Falkland Is., 37
False Bank grounds, 33
Farish, John T., 17
Fayal, Azores, 34, 36, 69, 99
Fickett, S. & F., 18
Food, aboard ships, 24-25, 34-37, 56, 66, 80
Fox Is., Alaska, 85
Foyn, Svend, 114, 115
France, 26, 109, 112
Friends of the American System, 7

"Gaily the Troubadour," 54
Galapagos Is., Ecuador, 34, 37
Gardiner, Warren, 99
George, Thomas, 73
Georgia, Gulf of, B. C., Can., 116
Germany, 26
Gilbert Is., Pac., 26
Good Hope, Cape of, 13, 39, 45, 56, 59
Grant, Capt. William J., 65

INDEX

147

Gravesend, Eng., 70
Gravesend Bay, N. Y., 8
Great Britain, 4, 83
Great International Fisheries Exhibition 1883, 118
Green, Ann Eliza, 117
Green, Capt. H., 105
Green, Capt. H. J., 40, 59, 99
Greenland, 108
Greenland Sea, 107-108
Greenport, L. I., 8, 123
Griswold, N. L. & G., 17
Guam, Mariana Is., 56, 63, 95
Gumshar, B. C., Can., 117

Hackstaff, Capt. William G., 20-21
Hafnarfjördur, Iceland, 114
Hale, Ebenezer, 18, 122
Hale, Josiah L., 7
Hale, Thomas, 18
Hale, Capt. Thomas, Jr., 18
Hall, Joshua, 18, 122
Hallock, Capt. Frederick M., 89, 90
Halsey, Capt. Edward, 30, 39, 55-56, 59, 121
Hammer, Capt. O. C., 114
Harris, J. Arthur, 120
Haverstraw, N. Y., 7
Hawaii, 26, 34, 35, 63, 90, 91, 92, 93, 94, 96, 101, 116
Hedges, Capt. Hiram B., 35, 44, 59, 100
Hedges, Capt. William, 44, 99
Henderson, Anderson & Co., 114
Hernaman, Capt. Richard T., 70-71
Hewlett, Charles, 123
Hewlett, Jacob C., 5
Hewlett, William M., 6
Hewlett-Jones grist mill, 24
Hidalgo, Joseph, 56
Hobart, Tas., Aust., 63, 103
Holdridge, Capt. Henry, 21
Holland, 112
Hong Kong, B.C.C., 106
Honolulu, Hawaii, 34-35, 36, 39, 51, 56, 61, 63, 65, 66, 67, 84, 86, 91, 94, 96, 97, 101, 104, 105, 106, 115, 116, 121, 123, 124
Hood, Daniel, 21
Horn, Cape, 13, 34, 101
Howell, John, 53
Howland, G. & M., 100
Hudson, N. Y., 16

Hudson Bay, Can., 3, 107
Hudson River, N. Y., 16
Hunt, Harry, 9
Hunter, Gov. Robert, 8
Huntington, L. I., 10n., 11

Iceland, 102, 108, 108n., 110, 111, 113-115
Ilha Grande, Brazil, 69
Illustrated London News, 82
Indian Ocean, 13, 33, 34, 69, 70, 100, 127
Indians, 5, 8, 14, 26, 42, 94, 116, 117
International Whaling Commission, 3
Ireland, 26
Islands, Bay of, N. Z., 53, 63, 99

Jamaica, W. I., 111
Japan, 4, 67
Japan Sea, 33, 66, 86, 95
Jessup, Isaac, 37, 53, 56, 57
Jones, Charles H., 7, 22, 122
Jones, John D., 122, 125
Jones, John H., 6, 7, 8, 10, 11, 12, 14, 17, 18, 24, 29, 30, 35, 51, 65, 91, 97, 122, 124, 127
Jones, Joseph, 122
Jones, Joshua, 7, 22, 99
Jones, Thomas, 8
Jones, Townsend, 11
Jones, Walter R., 6, 7, 10, 12, 14, 18, 22, 51, 82, 97, 105, 122, 124, 127
Jones, William H., 6, 7, 10
Jones brothers, 8, 9, 10, 14, 22, 25, 97
Jones general store, 6, 12, 25, 29-30, 127
Judson, Hon. Andrew T., 92

Kamchatka Pen., U.S.S.R., 66, 68, 86
Kamchatka Sea, 39
"Kanakas," 26, 35, 41, 52, 56, 58, 67, 94, 120, 121
Kanaka Charles, 56
Kanaka Tom, 56
Kerguelen Is., Ind. O., 62
Kilyas, David, 59
Kings Mills (Gilbert) Is., Pac., 58
Kodiak Is., 33, 66
Kuril Is., U.S.S.R., 39, 95

Lahaina, Hawaii, 51, 63, 116
Lamburd, 71, 74-77
Lamont, Hugh H., 117
Land, Capt. John, 17
Lang & Delano, 125
Lapland, Eur., 108
Leavitt, David, 122
Leek, Capt. Samuel, 61, 62
Leland, Jennison A., 17
LePont, Jo, 121
Lilliendahl, G. A., 112-115
Lisbon, Port., 111
Lisle, John, 99
Liverpool, Eng., 14, 19, 20, 21, 110, 114, 126
London, Eng., 64, 71, 82, 118
Long Island, N. Y., 8, 14, 21, 25, 123
Long Island Biological Assn., 127
Long Island Sound, 30, 119
Long Islander, Huntington, L. I., 120, 123
Lorient, France, 108, 117
"Loss of the *Albion,*" 54
Louisiana & New York Line, 19
Ludlow, Capt. Isaac, 69, 78-83
Ludlow, Phoebe, 82
Lutwyche, Alfred, 74-78

Magdalena Bay, Mex., 126-127
Mahan, George, 98-99
Main St., Cold Spring Harbor, L. I., 45, 100, 120, 127
Manchester, Eng., 110
Mangaia, Cook Is., 61, 62
Marias Is., Mex., 59
Matinecock Indians, 5
Mauritius, Ind. O., 81-82
Maury, Lt. Matthew F., U.S.N., 107-108
Mazatlan, Mex., 117
McDermot, John, 60
McGann, James, 60
McGarr, William, 42, 99
McManus, Richard, 21
McManus, Robert, 21, 22
Melville, Herman, 84
Merchants' Line, 22
Mersey River, Eng., 21
Mexico, 114
Miller, D. S., 122
Mills; woolen, 6, 7, 24; flour, 6, 24, 25, 127
Mississippi River, 19

Mittimore, Andrew W., 18
Moby Dick, 84
Moore, Charles B., 122
Morning Chronicle, London, Eng., 82
Mulford, Capt. Jeremiah, 29, 100 101
Murphy, Dr. Robert Cushman, 126

Nanaimo, B. C., Can., 116
Nantucket, Mass., 4, 84
Natchez, Miss., 22
National Observatory, 107
Negroes, 26
Netherlands, 4
New Bedford, Mass., 4, 50, 60, 66, 68, 84, 89, 91, 94, 95, 96, 99, 100, 112, 126
New England, 26
New Line, 19
New London, Conn., 10, 14, 25, 62, 95, 107
New Orleans, La., 13, 18-20
New Suffolk, L. I., 123
New York, N. Y., 5, 6, 7, 8, 9, 12, 14, 16, 17, 18, 19, 20, 21, 22, 23, 25, 82, 93, 94, 96, 105, 106, 108, 112, 115, 119, 120, 124, 125
New York State, 16, 26
New York State Legislature, 10, 11
New York State Supreme Court, 11
New Zealand, 13, 26, 33, 66, 99, 106
Newburgh, N. Y., 16
Newbury, Mass., 18
Newfoundland, Can., 21
North Pacific Ocean, 13, 33, 38, 39, 50, 94, 102-103, 107
North Shore, L. I., 5
North West Coast (Alaska), 17, 33, 99, 116
Norway, 4, 102, 112
Norwich, Conn., 50, 109
Nova Scotia, Can., 26
Novaya Zemlya, U.S.S.R., 109

Oakley, Zophar B., 10
O'Brien, John, 60
Okhotsk Sea, 33, 34, 51, 68, 95
O'Maley, Richard, 60
Oporto, Port., 110
Ormesby, Capt. Hiram, 35
Ostrov Iony, U.S.S.R., 95
Oyster Bay, Town, L. I., 10n., 11n.

INDEX

Pacific Ocean, 16, 33, 34, 63, 64, 67, 85, 100, 103, 106, 108, 126, 127
Packets; New Orleans, 13, 17, 18-20, 22; Record runs: *Huntsville,* 19-20, *Sheffield,* 21; Transatlantic, 13, 14, 20-21
Palmer, Capt., 21
Palmer, Capt. Nathaniel B., 19
Peace and Plenty Inn, 10n.
Peconic, L. I., 117
Pell, 79
Penney, Capt. George, 39, 58
Pennsylvania, 125
Penzhinskaya, Gulf of, U.S.S.R., 51
Pernambuco, Brazil, 36
Perry, Commodore Matthew C., U.S.N., 67
Petropavlovsk-Kamchatskiy, U.S.S.R., 103
Pfau, 73
Philadelphia, Penna., 10, 14
Phinney, Capt. Edward B., 100
Pierson, Charles, 29, 94
Pierson, Elihu, 29, 94
Pierson, Capt. Samuel B., 29, 67, 94-97
Pierson, Theodore, 29, 94
Polk, Pres. James, 17
Polynesia, 13
Polynesian, Honolulu, Hawaii, 124
Popham, Capt. Charles W., 21
Port Louis, Mauritius, 80, 82
Portland, Me., 21
Portugal, 26
"Portugees," 29, 35, 41, 100, 101, 120
Post & Sherry, 86
Post vs. Jones (court case), 91-94
Poughkeepsie, N. Y., 10, 16
Poughkeepsie Whaling Co., 16

Queen Charlotte Sound, B.C., Can., 116
Queenstown Cobh, Ireland, 109

Rarotonga, Cook Is., 61, 62
Rash, Daniel B., 60
Red Star Line, 20
Reeve, Edbert A., 31
Reeves, Charles H., 86, 88, 89, 91
Robertson, John M., 14
Rocket harpoon, 112-118; early experiments leading to, 108-112
Rogers, Daniel, 10

149

Rogers, John Henry, 83
Romer Shoal, N.Y., 21
"Rotten Row," 62
Royal Arsenal, Woolwich, Eng., 114
Royal Institution for the Preservation of Lives from Shipwreck, 83
Roys, Capt. Andrew, 113
Roys, John, 113, 114
Roys, Marie Salliord, 117
Roys, Philander, 117
Roys, Capt. Samuel, 66, 113
Roys, Capt. Thomas Welcome, 34, 39, 50, 56-57, 59-60, 66, 84, 102-118, 123
Roys, Capt. William Henry, 113
Roys whale, 107
Russia, 109

Sag Harbor, L.I., 4, 8, 9, 23, 25, 29, 34, 47, 53, 67, 69, 86, 89, 92, 99, 102, 104, 105, 109
St. Helena Is., Atlantic O., 33, 39, 62, 63
St. John's Church, 119, 127
St. Jona Is. (Ostrov Iony), U.S.S.R., 95
St. Paul's Is., Ind. O., 70, 71
St. Vincent, W.I., 111
Sakhalin Is., U.S.S.R., 95
Salliord, Marie, 117
San Cristobal, Solomon Is., Pac., 66
San Diego, Calif., 117
San Francisco, Calif., 33, 60, 96, 105, 115, 116, 117
Sayre, William, 88, 91
Scammon, Capt. Charles M., U.S.R.M., 107
Scoresby, Capt. William, 107
Scotland, 26, 113
Scrimshaw, 48, 54-55
Scudder, Nathaniel, 42
Serrill, Capt. James, 14
Setauket, L. I., 126
Seydhisfjördhur, Iceland, 113
Shapter, Capt. Thomas B., 22
Shinnecock Indians, 26
Ships:
 C.S.S. Alabama, 125
 Albion, 54
 Alexander Mansfield, 53
 Alice, 15, 18, 39, 50, 52, 56, 58, 68-69, 96, 98, 107, 123, 124, 126

INDEX

American Eagle, 6, 30
Andrew Hicks, 50
Ann Alexander, 84
Ann McKimm, 17
Anne, 116
Arabella, 69
Barclay, 15n.
Birmingham, 20
Britannia, 20
Byzantium, 116-117
Charles Carrol, 96
Cicero, 96
Columbus, 21
Creole, 18
Daisy, 126
Daniel Wood, 50
Edgar, 14, 21-22, 29, 85, 94-97, 125
Elbe, 16
Elizabeth Frith, 86, 88-93
Emma, 115-116
Enterprise, 95
Essex, 84
Florida, 20
France, 53
Frances Palmer, 96
George Washington, 21
Hannah Brewer, 62-63
Hannibal, 107-108, 117
Hero, 19
Hudson, 102
Huntsville, 15, 18-20, 29, 34, 35, 44, 51, 56, 65, 99, 103, 107, 120, 121, 123, 124, 125
Inga, 66-67
Java, 100
Jefferson, 95
Jireh Swift, 96
John Sugars, 71
John & Winthrop, 100
Josephine, 102
Junior, 89-92, 94
Kathleen, 84
King Fisher, 95
Lagoda, 91
Louisville, 18
Manchester, 20
Manhattan, 67
Matilda Sears, 100
Meridian, 70-83
Monmouth, 8, 9, 11, 14, 15, 25, 30, 31, 33, 35, 39, 41, 44, 55, 59, 62-63, 64, 69-70, 78, 79, 80, 82, 83, 121, 122-123, 125-126

Montreal, 91
Nashville, 18
Natchez, 18
Nathaniel P. Tallmadge, 13, 15, 16-17, 24, 29, 32, 39, 44, 49, 57, 58, 97, 99, 100-101, 121, 124, 125
Neptune, 103
Norwood, 17
Oliver Crocker, 68-69
Oscar, 69
Pacific (packet), 20
Pacific (steamship), 109
Pacific (whaler), 110-111
Panama, 89, 90, 92, 93
Pequod (fictional), 84
Pocahontas, 53
Polar Star, 68-69
Reindeer, 113
Richmond, 15, 17, 85-94, 125
Rodman, 60-61
Roman II, 95
San Francisco, 7
Sheffield, 14, 15, 20-21, 30, 31, 37, 39, 40, 44, 45, 50, 53, 54, 56, 57, 58, 59, 66, 84, 98, 99, 102, 105-107, 108, 121, 123, 124, 125
C.S.S. *Shenandoah,* 125
Silas Holmes, 20
Sileno, 113
Splendid, 14, 15, 17, 35, 67, 94, 97, 98, 121, 124, 125
Steypireydur, 113, 114
Sultana, 20
Superior, 34, 39, 86, 103-105
Thomas Roys, 114
Tuscarora, 10, 11, 13, 14, 15, 33, 35, 38, 39, 40, 45, 52, 56, 59, 60-62, 97, 124
Vigilant, 113, 114
Visionary, 113
U.S.S. *Warren,* 60
Washington, 86
William Byrnes, 20
Wm. F. Safford, 109-111
Young Phoenix, 96
Shipwrecks, 84-97
Siberia, U.S.S.R., 87, 103, 104
Siberians, 39, 45
Sierra Nevada mtns., Calif., 124
Slops chest, 30
Smith, Capt. 62
Smith, Capt. C. R., 22

INDEX

Simth, Capt. Franklin F., 14
Smith, Capt. Freeman H., 29, 34, 51, 103
Smith, Henry, 59
Smith, Capt. Richard P., 30, 98
Smith, Stephen, 20
Smith, William, 78
Smith & Dimon, 20
Snow, Charles, 71, 72, 73, 81, 83
Soldering, Capt., 103
"A Soldier's Gratitude," 54
South America, 100
South Atlantic Ocean, 8, 33, 34, 38, 63, 103, 125, 126
South Georgia, 110
South Pacific Ocean, 26, 40, 60, 106, 125
South Pacific Is., 35, 36
South Seas Is., 35, 36, 66, 103
South Seas whale grounds, 62, 63
South Shore, L.I., 8
South Street, N.Y.C., 7
Southwark, Philadelphia, Penna., 14
Soviet Union, 4
Spain, 26
Spall, Capt. George H., 22
Spitsbergen Is., Norway, 109
Starbuck, Alexander, 15n.
"Stone Jug," 120
Stonington, Conn., 19
Stratton, Sam, 101
Suffolk County, L.I., 8
Sydney, N.S.W., Aust., 62, 63, 67, 70, 71, 82, 83

Tahiti, 26, 53, 63, 125
Talcahuano, Chile, 34, 35, 100
Tallmadge, Nathaniel P., 16-17
Third Line, 22
Thurston, Ezekial, 21
Topping, Capt. Richard S., 8
Towns, Robert, 62
Trinity Church, N.Y.C., 7
Tristan da Cunha Is., So. Atl., 13, 33, 63, 69
Tulloch, Edward, 73, 81
Tuscarora Indians, 14

Underhill, Samuel J., 10
Union Line, 22
U.S. Circuit Court, S.D., N.Y., 92
U.S. Congress, 9

U.S. Court, S.D., N.Y., 91-92, 94
U.S. Customs, 5, 9, 9n.
U.S. Supreme Court, 85, 93, 94
U.S. Treasury Dept., 9

Valparaiso, Chile, 34, 59, 125
Vancouver Is., B.C., Can., 117
Victoria, B.C., Can., 115, 116-117
Victoria Whaling Adventurers Co., 115

Wales, U.K., 26
Wall St., N.Y.C., 7
War of 1812, 113
Washington, D.C., 9, 15n., 112
Washington Terr., 116
Wayne County, N.Y., 102
Webb & Allen, 18
Weeks, 44
West, Capt. William, 14
West Hills, L.I., 10n.
West Indies, 5, 111
Western Is. (Azores), 33
Western Pacific Ocean, 86
Whaleboats, 32-33, 41
Whales: capturing, 41-44; conservation, 3-4; processing, 46-50; types, 33
Whaleships: cost, 23; outfitting, 23-30
Whaling: Colonial, L.I., 8, 11; modern, 3-4
Whaling grounds, 33, 34, 38
Whaling Museum Society, Inc., 126-127
White, Capt. Eli, 58, 59
Whitworth, Sir Joseph, 109, 110, 111
Willets, Amos, 12, 120-121
Willets, Samuel, 12, 120-121
Willets & Co., 65, 120-121, 122, 124-125
Williams, William, 35
Willis, Henry, 10
Winters, Charles, 86
Winters, Capt. Jonas, 86, 88, 89, 90
Winters, Capt. Philander, 85-89, 91-92
Winters, Silas, 86
Wisconsin, 16
Wood, Capt. Daniel D., 68-69
Woolwich, Eng., 114
Worthington, Leonard, 72, 81

639.2   Schmitt.
S355   Mark well the whale.
c.1

Date Due

18079	27 Jun '73	450731	20 Apr '78
15546	19 Nov '73	49179	29 Nov '78
26857	18 Dec '73	DEC 2 6	APR 0 5 1981
t 27846	20 Sep '74	APR 2 3	DEC 1 4 1988
23227	12 Nov '74	MAY 3 1	
BK	11 Apr '75	MAY 0 7 1983	OCT 2 3 1989
36789	15 Apr '76	NOV 2 3 1994	
40203	23 Jun '76	APR 2 0 1980	
36383	5 Aug '76	AUG 1 2 2002	
47556	19 Jan '78		

BRODART PRINTED IN U.S.A.

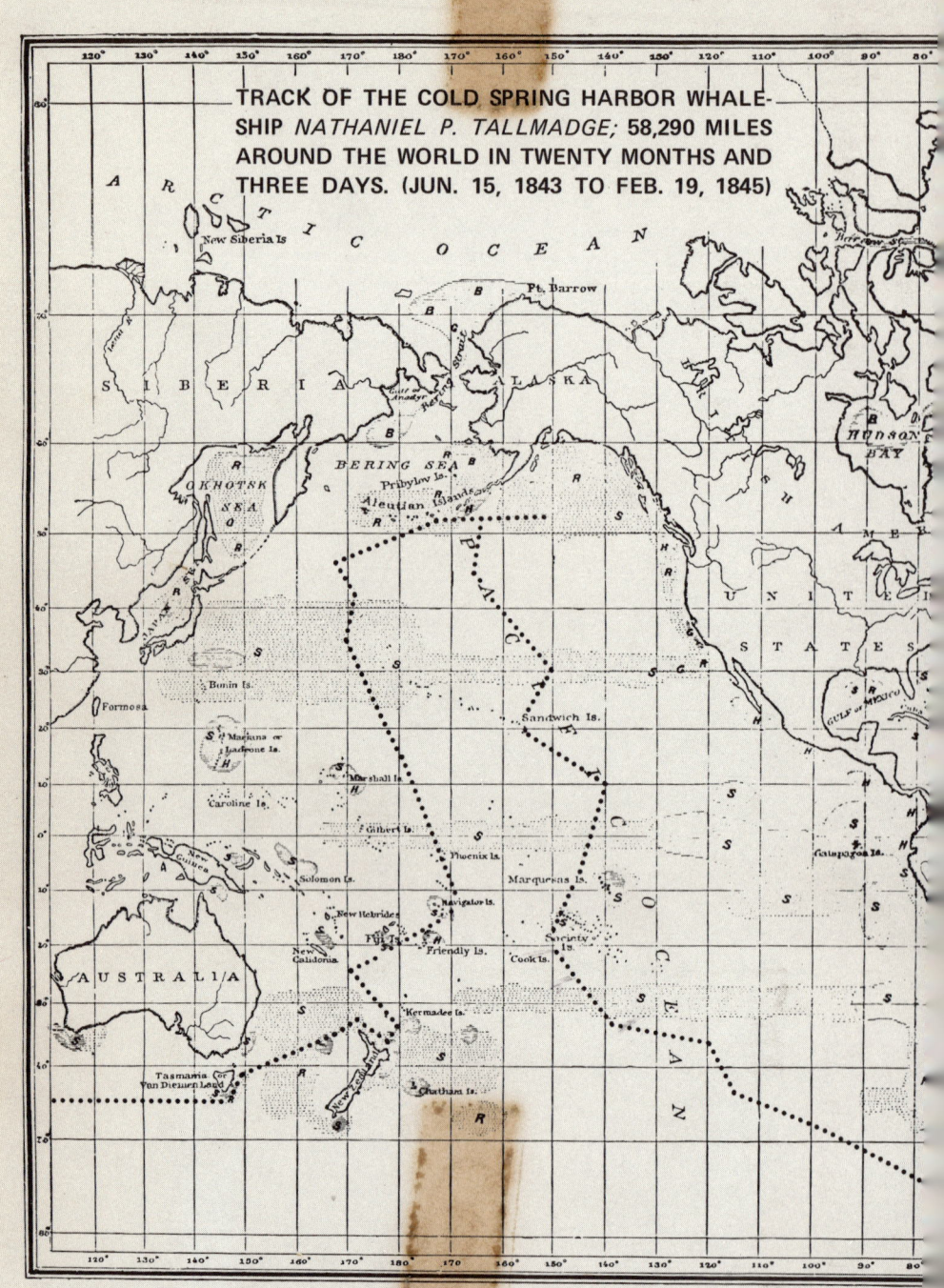

TRACK OF THE COLD SPRING HARBOR WHALE-
SHIP *NATHANIEL P. TALLMADGE;* 58,290 MILES
AROUND THE WORLD IN TWENTY MONTHS AND
THREE DAYS. (JUN. 15, 1843 TO FEB. 19, 1845)

Base chart prepared by U.S. Fish Commission, 1887.